Au

Writing this book was inspired by *Lucky's Story*, which is about the amazing survival of Lucky who was trapped in a container crossing the Atlantic.

You may have already read about Lucky in my book *More Cat Stories*, but in case you haven't, it's included in this collection of true cat stories as a tribute to the courage of cats everywhere.

TRUE CAT STORIES

Stella Whitelaw

With very best wishes

Stella Whitelaw.

ARROW BOOKS

Arrow Books Limited
62–65 Chandos Place, London WC2N 4NW

An imprint of Century Hutchinson Limited

London Melbourne Sydney Auckland
Johannesburg and agencies throughout
the world

First published 1986

Illustrated by Lesley Craig

Photoset by Rowland Phototypesetting Ltd
Bury St Edmunds, Suffolk
Printed and bound in Great Britain by
Anchor Brendon Limited, Tiptree, Essex

ISBN 0 09 943290 0

*To Cousin Edna
and the elusive Katie*

Contents

Acknowledgements	viii
Splodge and Tab	9
The Stowaway	18
Nirvana	27
White Tiger	31
The Uninvited Guest	38
Lucky's Story	46
Churchill's Cats	56
The Highland Hunter	65
Top Cat	73
Hamlet on West Forty-fourth Street	83
Scraps	91
Rescue in Venice	102
Cat in Court	110
The Siamese Traveller	117
Cat Knievel	129
Susie's Letters	137
Star Struck	153
Cloud Eight	162
Ad Infinitum	167

ACKNOWLEDGEMENTS

With many thanks for so much encouragement and help to Mrs Barbara Bristow, Mrs Janet Gadd, Mrs Marion Porter, Dr Theodore Reed, Mrs P. Knight, Miss Linda Thomas, Miss Grace Hamblin, Mr Peter Fairlie, Mr Andrew Anspach, Mrs Olivia Slobbé, Mrs Helena Sanders, Mrs Jane Froud, Mrs Judith Malet, Mrs Val Andrews, Mrs Joan Toy, Miss Theodora Croucher, Miss Beryl Reid, Miss Dorothy Wozniak – and all those who contributed to the 'Ad Infinitum' chapter.

Splodge and Tab

The strongly marked grey and black tabby was the wildest cat for miles around. No one could catch him or touch him. He prowled the neat Surrey gardens as if remembering the days when it was a primeval forest and ferals roamed in packs; or perhaps his ancestral memory went back to the century when huntsmen flew along the ridge of the North Downs led by their cruel king, a heavy man whipping his steaming horse.

Battles had been fought where there are now leafy suburban gardens, and a medieval cannon-ball had been unearthed near where the tabby sat, so still, like a statue, watching the family going about its tidy, methodical ways.

He did not know if he envied them, but something drew him to the family. It was more than curiosity. He was not starving. There were mice enough on the farm where he hung out. He needed this family but he was not sure why.

They tried to approach him but immediately his upper lip curled back in a ferocious snarl, a deep hiss coming from his throat. Then he was off like an arrow into the safety of the bushes. He watched from his hiding place as they searched for him, making soothing noises.

'Puss, puss, puss. Where are you?'

He stayed hidden. Eventually they gave up and went back indoors, but the woman returned with a saucer of milk, which she put down. He did not touch it.

She did not give up easily. She gave him a name.

'Tab, Tab, Tab,' she called now. But he made no move towards her. He came and sat and watched. If anyone came too near, he hissed, fangs bared.

She began to leave food. He had never smelt anything like it before. He could feel his resistance slipping as his salivary glands began to work and his stomach churned. How did she find such delicious food? There was none of it around the farm, only mice, dormice and moles. Sometimes he caught a squirrel, but their fur was so rough and harsh in his mouth. Once he had chased and pounced on a rabbit in the field behind the church . . . now that had been a feast. Perhaps this woman had been into the field chasing a rabbit . . .

He waited until she returned indoors, shutting the back door. She was watching from the kitchen window so he did not move. It was hours before he crept forward in the growing darkness and tentatively sniffed at the new food. It was good. He gulped it down and fled.

'Tab, here's your supper.'

She was there again the next evening with a saucer of food. It was not fair. Tab could not resist. But he did wait until all the humans had disappeared before he ate. This food was so much nicer than mice and so much easier to get. A plan formed in his mind.

One day he came to sit in the garden and watch, and he was not alone. He had brought another feral with him, a small black cat. She was a thin creature but her stomach was swollen with pregnancy.

It is thought that ferals always fight over food, but Tab allowed the black cat to feed first from the dish that had been left out. Then he finished off the remains. The female cat was too heavy to hunt now. Someone had to take care of her, so he had brought her to the family.

'Do you think it's his mate, or his sister?' they whispered. 'She's as wild as he is.'

'Perhaps they are just good friends.'

'I'll find a box and put it outside in the covered way. It's getting cold at nights,' said the woman. 'She may have her kittens here.'

Titch produced four kittens in the box . . . two grey, one black and a tabby. Tab grew more handsome in appearance despite his ragged cauliflower ear. The black markings were dense on his brown ground coat, the rings narrow and numerous; and his round face was fiercely protective. But he was affectionate towards the kittens and could be seen washing them occasionally.

Titch was a good mother, though she was even wilder than Tab. She reared her kittens well. But the road was a hazard she did not understand. As her kittens grew more independent she often left them to escape to the fields. It meant crossing the road. One day she did not make it.

Tab remained, thrown by the death of the female feral. He stood guardian over the kittens, disturbed to find that they were also disappearing from the box. They were being found good homes, civilised homes in houses with doors and windows and rules for cats. He did not know whether this was a good thing; it was not something he wanted for himself. He wanted freedom and life in the wild. But other cats seemed to like it and even thrived on domesticity. He had seen them cleaning their paws on doorsteps in the sunshine.

One of the grey kittens was a pretty long-haired fluffy creature with a fawn splodge on the side of its neck. The woman seemed to favour this kitten, picking it up and talking to it.

'Come along, Splodge,' she said. 'You're going to live with us. I think you'll like it.'

The kitten was quite happy with the idea. She liked the woman and the family of four children, and she took to living in the house with a natural grace.

Tab wandered back to the fields around the farm and

thought about this new development. Would the woman still put out those delicious saucers of food now that she had her own cat? Perhaps he would be back to catching mice and more mice. He roamed the North Downs wondering if the woman was catching rabbits for the grey kitten.

But he could not keep away. He came back and sat in their garden to watch the strange business of training the kitten. It required a lot of putting out and bringing in, and calling.

'Splodge, Splodge, Splodge . . . kitty, kitty, kitty.'

The woman pretended not to notice Tab though she was well aware that the feral was watching, almost camouflaged by the leafy shadows and ferns sprouting from the next door rockery. She was teaching the kitten to dig in the soft dry earth. Splodge was wriggling and rolling over in the dust on the garden path.

As they went indoors together, the woman looked over her shoulder, directly to where Tab sat immobile in the shadows.

'Hello, Tab,' she said. 'I'll put your supper out in a minute.'

He snarled and hissed though she was nowhere near him.

No one knew that Tab's eyesight was not as good as it used to be. He thought perhaps the world had gone hazy and that it was an atmospheric change due to the weather. He had always been able to roam and climb as vigorously and fearlessly as any feral; nothing was too high or too difficult.

There was a willow tree in the next door garden. He had climbed it many times. Sometimes he had climbed to the topmost branches so that he could see into the upper windows, watching the family at their curious activities.

This day he climbed to the top of the willow, leaping with ease from branch to branch, scattering the twittery birds and hovering bumblebees with a lash of his tail.

12

Perhaps today they would be gardening or washing the car; or the boys would be kicking a football around in some game in which he longed to join.

As he watched, he slowly noticed that this atmospheric change in the weather which was affecting his eyes seemed much worse today. He could hardly see what was going on below. Then he realised that he could not see the other branches of the tree either; that it was all a confused pattern of changing shapes and shadows that bore no relation to the tree which he had climbed.

He waited, hoping that the mist would clear. He sent silent distress signals into the air waves. But who would hear him? He had no friends.

Splodge was by now almost fully grown, a beautiful cat with a long silky grey and fawn coat and big amber eyes. She summed up the situation at once, and climbed the tree with the agility of youth. She came to within a few feet of the feral cat and miaowed.

Tab turned his head towards the noise. He vaguely saw the young cat, recognised its smell. It was one of those kittens, the one that went to live in the house. He had observed its antics as it was put out and called in. But it was the kitten of the black feral and therefore not alien.

Splodge miaowed again and moved along the branch so that the long swaying leaves made a noise. Tab realised that here was an opportunity to descend, even if only to one branch lower. He jumped.

The family watched from a window. They were amazed, calling to each other to come and watch.

'Just look at this. Splodge is helping old Tab get down the tree. I've never seen anything like it. Look, she's actually guiding him . . .'

It was true. Branch by branch, with infinite patience, the young cat was showing the feral where to jump, guiding him down a safe route through the swaying and rustling tree. Splodge jumped to the ground and looked back. Tab followed, feeling the earth beneath his paws

13

with a wave of relief. The two cats looked at each other, and then with one bound Tab disappeared into the bushes and ran home to the farm.

The family made a great fuss of Splodge, with much stroking and patting and a saucer of cream from the top of the milk. She was a heroine.

'Clever Splodge. Well done, Splodge.'

'Old Tab didn't seem very grateful.'

'How can you tell if a cat is grateful?'

They wondered if Tab would now seek different pastures, but after a few days he turned up again. Still watching and waiting and eating whatever was left out for him when everyone had gone.

If there was a rapport between the two cats, it was unspoken. There was no obvious comradeship. But there was a degree of communication indiscernible to humans.

The woman was quietly ironing one afternoon by the window that looked onto the back garden. There was no one else about and she was making very little noise. Through the glass serving partition into the kitchen, she had a good view of the back door.

Splodge came in through the open door, hesitated and looked back. To her amazement, the woman then saw the striped front paws and flat nose of the wild feral. He peered into the kitchen as if into another world.

She expected him to immediately turn tail and race back into the garden, but Tab's long white whiskers were twitching with all the new smells, and curiosity overcame his fear. Splodge moved a few paces over the polished lino and looked back again. Tab followed slowly until the whole length of his body was over the step. But that was as far as he was going.

The woman held her breath. Splodge had achieved the introduction where they had all failed. The wild cat was actually in the kitchen.

Tab looked around with wide-eyed wonder at all the strange things – cupboards and kettles, sinks and saucepans. He had never seen such objects and had no idea what people wanted them for.

Splodge moved a few more steps and looked back as if to say, 'come on'. Tab followed Splodge into the sitting room, amazed by the softness of the carpet under his paws and the warmth from the fire. He saw the woman outlined against the window, but it was as if she was just another object. He was walking through a wonderland, treading carefully, unsure of everything, tense, but following Splodge like an open-mouthed tourist through a palace.

Splodge took Tab on a complete tour of the house. They went upstairs, into every bedroom, even the bathroom. There was not one nook or cranny that Tab did not peer into. It was the most amazing adventure of his life. He could not believe all that he saw.

But it was also quite overwhelming. There was so much that he did not understand, so many things that puzzled him. He looked at Splodge regretfully. This could never be his world. His life was the open fields, the wild and wet woods, the stream that threaded through the gardens, and the echoing barns around the farm. He could not stand four walls.

He finished the tour politely enough. No panic or mad rush to escape outside. He left as quietly as he had entered. Splodge sat down and began to wash her long pinky-tinged fur. She had done her best. She had been a good hostess, shown the visitor around, and when he wanted to leave, she had let him go.

The woman was speechless. She had never seen anything quite so moving between two animals . . . first the intelligent rescue from the tree, and now the guided tour of the house.

She held the beautiful, purring grey cat in her arms, thinking how strange it was that in a world full of bitter fighting and global tragedies, two cats, one wild and one domestic, could actually show some concern for the other.

15

Then Splodge disappeared. At first they thought that she was just being wilful and staying out all night. But night turned into the next day and she did not appear. Day one grew into day two and the woman was sick with worry. There was a busy blind junction at the end of the road and she remembered little Titch. A stream of lorries came from the chalk pits that were being dug out of the North Downs. And not far away, behind an embankment, the new motorway thundered with vehicles day and night.

Days turned into weeks, then a month. Tab still came to their garden. He saw their distress, but how could he tell them anything? He was only a cat. He was powerless. He could not take the place of Splodge. He could only try with his continuing presence to give them some comfort, little as it was.

The woman continued to put out food for Tab in the cold and frosty December days.

'Here you are, Tab,' she called out, but her voice was without joy.

It was five weeks since Splodge had disappeared and it was Christmas Eve. Although they had searched around and asked neighbours and given the police a description, there was no news and they had given up hope. They could only cross their fingers that death had been kind and that she had not been stolen for her beautifully coloured coat.

School had broken up and the younger son was in the kitchen. He was looking out of the window, thinking of what he had yet to do for Christmas, when a grey shadow crossed his vision. A cat was strolling nonchalantly up the garden path, its long tail sweeping the stones.

'Mum, Mum,' he called out. 'Come here! There's Splodge, I'm sure. She's coming up the garden.'

The woman had never taken the stairs so quickly. She flew down them, her heart in her mouth. Could it be . . . could it be their Splodge, or was it just some other cat that looked like her in the gathering gloom?

Her son opened the kitchen door and the grey cat sauntered in, slightly overdoing the casual act. She went over to her chair, jumped up onto it and sat down as if nothing had happened.

It was Splodge, thinner, a little bedraggled, her lovely grey and fawn fur dirty and tangled; but it was the best Christmas present the family had ever had.

Tab sat outside in the garden, the frosty stars bright in the December sky. He had watched the cameo of the return and was satisfied that the family were reunited.

Only Splodge and Tab knew where the grey cat had been all that time. Perhaps Tab had taken Splodge on a tour of his world, through the acres of fields and woods. Perhaps Splodge had felt the stirring of her ancestors' blood and tasted the delights of freedom. Perhaps she had forgotten about the family in the heady joy of running wild.

It may have been the cold that drove her back to her chair and the fireside. The diet of mice could have palled and become hard to find. Perhaps she longed for a dish of chicken or liver.

Or perhaps Tab had brought her back. No one knows and no one would ever know.

The Stowaway

(Adapted from an account by Mrs Janet Gadd)

The kitten was being brought home by car. He had never been in one before, and it was a highly alarming experience. He threw himself dramatically at the windows in an attempt to escape from this monster.

There was pandemonium. His tiny white paws clawed from window to window, accompanied by terrified mews. He had come from a semi-wild cat family owned by the village butcher. Some of the litter were too wild to be caught.

'Got him,' said Mum, throwing her cardigan over the kitten like a matador. 'He's as wild as a tiger. And he looks like one too. We'll just have to call him Tiger.'

So Tiger he became, but only by name and not by nature. Love tamed him and he matured into a friendly family cat, sharing the Roberts' home with another cat and four dogs, living in the beautiful seaside village of Penmaenmawr in North Wales.

He developed a penchant for sleeping next door. Many times Janet Gadd went to her front door to fetch in the milk and found Tiger asleep on the doormat or curled up among a pile of leaves that had blown into the porch. His favourite sleeping place was in the basket of a bike stored in the garage.

She had several bikes, for Janet and Harold Gadd are members of the Long Sutton and District Veteran Cycle Club. They own several veteran bikes, including a rare 1877 penny farthing.

In the middle of August 1985, the club was invited to ride and display their cycles at the annual Vintage Vehicle Rally at Rickinghall Inferior, Suffolk. The Gadds usually drive the three hundred miles overnight to avoid the heavy North Wales holiday traffic, but that Thursday evening the fuel tank was reading low and the nearest all-night filling station was some fifty miles away. They decided to postpone their departure, but packed their car and roof-rack with the bikes ready for an early start the next morning.

First their tent went on the roof in front of the extra-long rack. Then a canvas-covered bike went on the rack, with the penny farthing secured on top of the lot.

It was a clear summer's night when Tiger took his usual leisurely after-supper walk. He had had a lovely day playing with seven-year-old Stuart and now he was ready for a little snooze. He liked interesting new places. He nosed around the Gadds' garden, digging up a few bedding plants. He approved of the Gadds even though they did not have a cat. Perhaps that was why he liked them.

He explored a few of his old haunts but for some reason they all seemed boring. He fancied somewhere really new. Something a little out of the ordinary.

Janet and Harold left early on the Friday morning, one of those dewy-fresh mornings that make one wish for the incentive to get up at dawn every morning. They drove into the ancient town of Conwy, past the brooding castle and over the famous Telford bridge. The narrow streets were already traffic-jammed, and they stopped for petrol as soon as they could.

Tiger opened one eye. A red traffic light stared at him.

19

It was very strange. The lights began to blink, then moments later he was being jolted around and he dug his claws into some fabric to keep his balance. What on earth was happening? He hung on as he was carried away, the wind whistling through his fur. He gritted his teeth and shut his eyes against the rush of air, finding it difficult to breath.

He squinted sideways. Trees, houses, shops sped past. It was both terrifying and exhilarating at the same time. Tiger clung on, keeping his head down to reduce the wind resistance. So much was happening he could not take it all in. Up and down, this way and that way. He felt as if he were on a roller-coaster, only he didn't know what a roller-coaster was.

Daringly he peered about, trying to get his bearings, to make some sense. Where was he? He had vague memories of a journey once before, many years ago, when he had fought to get free, but that had been different, with walls he could not get through. Here it was all air – too much air, in fact. He was as free as a bird, but could he fly? The wind told him that he could, but a sense of self-preservation told him to stay where he was.

He sniffed, smelling salt in the air. He turned his head carefully, and there was an amazing sight before him. There were miles and miles of sparkling blue coming and going, breaking over the rocks and washing up on the shore. He had never seen such odd stuff, although he had sometimes smelt the same salt in the air at Penmaen-mawr. It was fascinating; all the little specks of white foam, begging to be played with. He longed to dip his paw in that tantalising straggling line of bubbles.

He was too absorbed to notice when they began to leave the sea road and turn inland. The scenery changed from blue to green and brown hills, then to red and grey. It was bewildering. He had never realised that there was anywhere else. He had thought the world began and ended in the village of Penmaenmawr. How wrong he had been.

They were slowing down now, circling in slow curves, but at the same time he could hear a growing roar. What could this noise be? It was louder than a tiger roaring in the jungle. The fur on his back began to tingle, to stand on end . . . it must be some enormous fearsome animal.

A vast grey path of asphalt stretched ahead, going far out of sight, and wider than anything he had ever seen before. It was packed with lines of cars and lorries, all travelling very fast.

As their speed increased, Tiger grew more and more alarmed. He dug his claws even further into the weave of the fabric and tucked his nose under his fur. There was nothing interesting to look at, only the roof-tops of cars, and besides, the great container lorries thundering by scared him stiff.

He felt he was spinning, disorientated, deafened by the traffic, speeding to some alien place where nothing would ever be the same again. Bridges rushed overhead, making his heart somersault.

'I could do with some coffee,' said Janet. 'And break-fast.'

'We'll pull off at the next service station,' said Harold. 'I'd like a stretch. We've done a hundred miles already so that's pretty good going.'

They turned off the M6 motorway at the Keele service station and drove slowly into the parking area, followed by another car. The passengers in this car were looking at them. Janet and Harold were used to this as their 1877 penny farthing always attracted attention wherever they went.

The passengers from the other car immediately came over to them.

'Do you know there's a cat on your roof?' they said.

'A penny farthing, you mean,' said Harold, blankly.

'No, it's a cat. Look for yourself.'

Janet got out of the car and looked at their car roof. She could not believe her eyes. Crouched among the bikes on their roof-rack was Tiger, their neighbours' cat.

His sweet tabby face peered down uncertainly. He was glad the jolting had stopped; that the rushing wind had stopped; that the world was steady at last. But he was still very wary.

He knew two of the people who were staring up at him in amazement. They lived next door. But there were a lot of other people, too, and he did not know any of them. He retreated further back among the folds of canvas.

'It's Tiger . . . Stuart's cat, from next door,' said Janet. 'I don't believe it. Good heavens, whatever do we do now?'

It took a combined effort to get Tiger off the roof-rack. He was obstinately reluctant to be moved from what now seemed a safe haven. Harold, who is not a cat-lover, tried to get hold of him from one side. Janet, who is shortish, was unable to reach him at all. The young men from the second car joined in the Tiger hunt. Tiger clung on grimly, determined to evade capture. At last he was dragged off the roof and bundled into the car. Janet went quite cold at the thought of Tiger charging down the M6.

'Now what are we going to do?' she said again.

Harold went into the service station shop to get a cardboard box, and Janet phoned home to her mother to get a message passed to the Roberts family next door.

'We can't come back with the cat,' said Janet on the phone. 'It's over a hundred miles. We'll have to keep Tiger with us for the weekend. We'll look after him the very best we can, but . . . you know, a cat in a strange place, and we're camping. And we've never looked after a cat before. There's a lot of problems and that's putting it mildly.'

'Are you sure you know what you're doing?' asked her mother, bewildered.

'Not really,' said Janet, running fingers through her tousled hair. 'But anyone ought to be able to look after one small tabby cat, oughtn't they?'

The news travelled round the car park like wildfire and

their estate car became the centre of attraction. The Gadds downed a quick breakfast while Tiger roamed around, restlessly investigating the back of their car.

As they sat in the front seats eating bacon sandwiches, a man came up to them. They wound down the window an inch.

'I believe you've found a cat,' he said. 'Would you like a box?'

They stared at him, unable to believe their good luck.

'I'm the driver of a removal van and I often have to move cats along with the furniture. There's a spare travelling box on the van. You can have it. I don't want it back.'

Tiger took an instant dislike to the box. He wanted to go back on the roof-rack. Why wouldn't they let him? It had been a bit precarious at times, but quite a thrill. He eyed Harold carefully, his wild-cat blood rising. Suddenly he saw his chance. He slithered through their hands like a furry eel and raced across the car park to freedom.

One of the helpful young men sprinted after him, cornering the cat with some fast thinking. Tiger growled.

'Oh no you don't,' said the young man, tucking the protesting tabby firmly under his arm. 'You've had enough adventures for one day.'

Tiger objected loudly to being put in the travelling box even though it was a good size. The car had to be repacked to make a space for it in the back.

'We'll have to stop somewhere and do some shopping,' said Janet raising her voice above Tiger's piercing miaows.

'I thought you'd done all the shopping before we left,' said Harold, putting the car in gear.

'Cat food!' said Janet with a grin. 'We've another mouth to feed.'

At Rickinghall, the organisers were preparing the site for the weekend rally. It was being held in a big field surrounded by trees and large enough to accommodate all the vehicles and tents.

'Hi there, Janet, Harold. Have a good journey?'

'You could say that,' said Janet. 'By the way, have you got a rabbit run?'

The organisers got asked for a lot of strange things, but this was a new one.

'A rabbit run?'

'Er . . . yes,' said Janet. 'You see, we've brought a cat with us.'

As their cycle club friends arrived, the search for some kind of cat run began. Tiger had to have some exercise without escaping. He could hardly live in their tent.

More friends, Nancy and Norman from Wisbech, arrived. They usually drove a small three-wheeler, but this weekend their son had brought them in his transit van.

'Oh, he's beautiful,' said Nancy, straight away taking him to her heart. She loved cats and Tiger knew it. 'He can live in our van. He can have the run of it during the day, and then sleep in his box in your car at night.'

Tiger settled to his new regime without a fuss, though he did a spectacular impersonation of a mad cat whenever they tried to put a collar and lead on him.

'He'll hurt himself,' they cried, abandoning the idea.

'Got a tiger in your tank?'

'Cat on a hot tin roof?'

Despite the jokes, Tiger enjoyed his celebrity status. Nancy made a fuss of him and he had a constant stream of visitors. He shared a fish-and-chip supper which the club organised as a Saturday evening event. It was bought from a little shop in the village and everyone saved him a morsel.

Sunday dawned cold and damp and the organisers of the rally eyed the grey skies with dismay. The thirty vintage cycles were given their final polish and oiling. The muddy field was going to be a problem.

Tiger heard his story being told over the Tannoy

system to all the visitors. He was an added attraction to the day, an extra dimension to the display . . . all those lovingly cared for vehicles from bygone eras and one small scrap of fur with an equal sense of self-preservation.

By mid-afternoon the sky had darkened and the drizzle turned to heavy rain. The club's cycles had been on display all day and members had taken part in an arena ride dressed in costumes suited to the year of their cycle. Now the crowds started to drift away, squelching over the mud.

Janet and Harold began to pack their bikes and camping gear, not forgetting to leave a space for Tiger's box. It was still raining hard and a strong wind was blowing. They needed all the help they could get to take the tent down and load it onto the roof-rack.

Tiger watched the preparation with curiosity. Was he going for a ride on the roof-rack again? He did not fancy the pelting rain, and the wind was already running cold fingers through his fur. But he trusted his new friends and waited to see what they were going to do with him.

Nancy gave him a big hug and kissed him, whispering into his ear all sorts of things that he understood perfectly. She would have liked to keep him.

'Come along, love,' said Norman, her husband. 'You can't adopt him.'

Finally Tiger was put into the travelling box and stowed away in the car. For once Tiger did not object. He was only too glad to be inside and not outside, watching the rain streaming down the windows. He enjoyed a service station stop for a drink and a stretch.

It was late evening when the Gadds drove into the road at the rear of their house.

Tiger had been dozing but suddenly he was alert. He leaped up, miaowing loudly, scratching, creating quite a commotion. As Janet opened the gates and Harold reversed the car into their garden drive, Tiger went wild. He knew exactly where they were. Hadn't he heard these noises a hundred times? Tiger threw himself about, pink mouth open in hoarse cries. He was desperate to get out, clawing at the wooden box.

The lights burned in the living room of the Roberts' house next door. They had spent an anxious weekend wondering if their pet would survive his camping holiday so far away. They had been waiting up and watching for the return of the Gadd's car.

Harold went to knock at the back door whilst Janet unlocked the tail-gate of their estate car and lifted out the box. She could hardly hold it as Tiger was throwing all his weight around in another exhibition of wildness. It would have been impossible to keep him in her arms.

As the Roberts opened their door, Janet lifted the wire mesh from the front of the box. Tiger shot out like lightning and raced across the garden, leaping over the wall in one high, effortless bound, straight into his house.

It was a beautiful sight. Janet felt a catch in her throat. That small creature had feelings. He was home. She could imagine the relief he felt after his strange adventure that weekend.

The Gadds went in next door for a cup of tea to tell the Roberts of Tiger's precarious one-hundred-mile ride on their roof-rack and the odd set of coincidences; stopping at a motorway service station fifty miles sooner than usual; the kindness of the removal-van driver; Nancy turning up in a much larger vehicle.

The next morning young Stuart woke up early. There was a familiar heaviness on his feet. Tiger was asleep at the end of his bed, nose tucked into his white bib, one paw curled over his face. The boy gave a wide smile. His cat was back, safe and sound.

Tiger refused to leave the house all that Monday. But come Tuesday . . . well, Tuesday was another day and there might be a new adventure around the corner.

Nirvana

The man stood staring out of the window. She had been gone some months now but still her fragrance lingered in the house. It was so empty and quiet. He was used to the two cats chasing each other up and down the stairs, the scampering feet on the wooden floor, the mock fights and hissing, then the chorus of catcalls when his wife took their supper out of the refrigerator.

He missed them curled together on his lap, replete and sleepy, each trying to push the other off, striving for extra space even in sleep. The two Burmese had been delightful innocent witnesses to his disintegrating life.

They had been a present to her, so she took them along with her other possessions. Taking the cats had been a knife turning in the wound. He was lonely. He found it difficult to work. He was a fine print photographer and worked at home. He was used to cats around, helping him at his desk, sometimes providing inspiration with their fine eyes and ethereal beauty. He could not bear life without having a cat.

Many miles away in Bedfordshire, a tiny female lilac Burmese kitten stirred in milky sleep. She had been bred from Bathsheba, a queen of rare beauty. There were four kittens in the litter, two small bundles of pink and grey fluff, two of the palest milky chocolate. They stretched their tiny pin-pointed claws into the warmth of their mother.

The breeder wanted a home for the lilac female with someone particularly loving and understanding who would give her the kind of extra care she would need.

'I've got to find someone very special for you, little one,' she told the kitten, examining the tiny creature again.

She was expecting a visitor that day, a man who had telephoned earlier asking particularly for a lilac Burmese female. He sounded weary but was prepared to drive a long way to see her kittens. She tried to explain the circumstances but he seemed undeterred. It was almost as if he was not listening to her.

'We used to have two Burmese but my wife's taken them with her,' he explained somewhat incoherently. 'I can't blame her, of course, they were a present to her, but I miss them . . . I've . . . I like . . .'

'You like having a cat around,' she finished for him. 'Especially a Burmese. I understand. They are so affectionate and make good pets. But this lilac female kitten, as I was saying, I don't know whether I should let her go . . .'

'I'd like to come and see her anyway. Please.'

She heard the despair and loneliness in his voice. It seemed this was another marriage break-up that had included not only the loss of a marriage partner, perhaps children, but also beloved pets. People rarely thought about the impact of losing pets.

The man must have started the long drive soon after talking to her on the telephone. He was a small, stocky man, dressed in jeans, sweater and sneakers, the past few months clearly etched on his face.

'Hello. You're here already,' she said in the doorway. 'What a long way to come. I hope you won't feel it's a wasted journey. Of course, I've other kittens – but only the one lilac female. Will you come this way, please?'

She took the man into the garden room, where the newest litter were lying in a heap on the sofa.

The man sat down on the floor in a slow movement of tired limbs folding up under him, wishing he had his camera with him. The heap of kittens rolled over and the lilac female detached herself. She pushed her way out of her squirming brothers and sister, an unsteady puff-ball of lavender fur, tiny tottering legs trampling over the vast expanse of the sofa towards the man.

They held their breath. They had done nothing to encourage the kitten, or attract her attention. The kitten went straight to the man. It seemed like an abyss between them, an unequal descent to reach the man's lap. There was nothing tentative about her movements or her determination. She was set on her objective . . . the man sitting on the floor.

To a kitten of that size it was a journey of immense proportions. But she made it, kneading the warmth of his sweater, a throaty purr growing in the fragile bird-like throat, blinking mistily into his eyes. The man was enchanted.

'But she's beautiful,' he said, unbelieving. 'How can you say she's deformed? She's quite perfect.'

The kitten had done her choosing and, satisfied with her choice, she curled up on his knee, exhausted by the effort. She went to sleep, trusting, ready to devote her life to his companionship.

'She certainly seems to like you. Rapport at first sight. It's amazing. I always think cats choose their owners, not the other way round.'

The man looked content, stroking the kitten. Before her eyes the breeder could see him relaxing. Animals could be therapeutic. The kitten was already weaving a spell round the man that would last for years.

'I'd like to have this kitten,' he said. Then he murmured into the soft fur. 'Princess Esmé . . . you will have a crystal bowl to drink water from, and one day, when you are used to a collar and lead, you will sail on the Thames with me . . .'

'I do insist on you thinking it over for a night,' she said.

'Just to make sure that her defect isn't going to worry you in the future. I can't take any chances with this kitten. She has to go to a very special person. Please look at her foot.'

She turned the sleepy bundle onto its back and found the front left foot, pushing aside the pale lavender fur. The kitten had two shell-pink pads and two claws instead of the normal pad and four toes.

It was a strange sight on the kitten, a rare deformity. Perhaps it would put the man off; perhaps he would find it distasteful and take one of the other kittens.

'I knew there was something,' he said mysteriously.

'I beg your pardon?'

'We have a bond,' he said.

He held out his left hand, pushing up the sleeve from his wrist. He turned his palm to the light, showing the line of a surgical scar.

'I was born with two thumbs.'

She let him take the kitten. There was simply no question about it. They were soul-mates. Some divine instinct had led them to each other.

Perhaps the kitten would change the man's future, open new doors, point new paths, make things happen that in some way would restore peace and tranquillity to his life. She knew the kitten would bring him happiness. It was written so.

White Tiger

Ebony was an ordinary black farm cat. He did not know
that he was fated to cross the path of a white tiger cub,
and that for a time they would live together.

The story really began ten years earlier when Dr
Theodore Reed journeyed to India to escort one of the
most beautiful and rare creatures in the world back to the
Smithsonian Institution's National Zoological Park in
Washington, DC.

Mohini, as she was called, translates as 'enchantress'
and she soon became one of the zoo's greatest attractions.
She bewitched people with her startling glacier blue eyes
and her white fur with its glamorous greyish-brown
stripes. She was a white tiger, a mutant from the better
known orange Bengal tiger.

It was not surprising that such an outstanding beauty
acted remote when it came to suitors. She did produce
three cubs with Samson, but the only white tiger cub
died of a virus.

Then she mated with Ramana and gave birth to a single
female white cub. The zoo was ecstatic about the new
arrival. The Indian Ambassador suggested a name for
her, Rewati, meaning 'a pure mountain stream'.

It was as if Mohini knew that her tiny cub was precious
and irreplaceable, very valuable and difficult to rear. She

began to lick the cub excessively and pace nervously around the cage, carrying the baby in her mouth. The zoo officials were worried. It was very odd behaviour. They felt the cub was in danger. The 420-pound tigress was normally a model mother, but the tiny bundle of 10,000-dollar fluff could so easily be crushed if Mohini was disturbed.

A decision had to be made.

Dr Reed took the cub home in his car. His wife, Elizabeth, was busy in the kitchen preparing a dinner party for fourteen guests. She was up to her elbows in stirring sauces and making dressings.

'Here's your new baby,' he said, putting the cub into her arms. 'We could turn one of the bedrooms into a nursery. She has to be in an incubator till she's stronger.'

Elizabeth looked at the small white kitten in her arms, totally bewildered. Incubator? Nursery? What on earth was she being let in for?

'But what are we going to feed her on?' she asked. 'Do we know about tiger's milk?'

'I can't find any information on tiger's milk,' said Dr Reed. 'The fat and protein content of the milk of big cats varies so much. We'll just have to use a commercial formula.'

Ebony watched the new arrival, his curiosity veiled with an aloof indifference. It was not unlike his own arrival at the house. He, too, had been smuggled upstairs.

The black cat was born in a barn on a busy farm. When the Reeds were on a visit there, Maryalice, their ten-year-old daughter, pleaded to be allowed to have one of the kittens, but her parents said no. The girl was very quiet on the drive home and her father thought she was sulking. But Maryalice was up to more than that. She had one of the kittens tucked inside her coat, a scrap of black fluff with a white spot on his chest, just to take the curse off.

Elizabeth was unable to resist the kitten when

Maryalice eventually confessed. It was a bright, intelligent little thing and they could not possibly take him back. Dr Reed gave in. He knew when he was beaten. They christened the kitten Ebony and he quickly became Elizabeth's cat, following her everywhere.

He loved to be vacuumed. Whenever he heard the cleaner, he came scampering over, arching his back in delicious anticipation. Ebony had the run of the house and the yard, as well as the neighbourhood. There was never any evidence that he caught mice or birds, but the chipmunks in the garden decided to make a rapid and permanent exit.

Ebony listened to the cub yowling that first night. It was an insistent sound. He heard two pairs of bare feet hurrying across to the new nursery. Ebony stood in the nursery doorway, glaring balefully as Elizabeth went to tend the tiny cub. Rewati was howling for a bottle and a dry blanket. It was the beginning of a regular three-and-a-half-hour routine of feeds.

Ebony had no objection to this middle-of-the-night routine as long as there was some milk in it for him. He padded into the kitchen, where Rewati's feed was being made up.

'I haven't forgotten you,' Elizabeth yawned. She sat down for a moment, cradling her head in her arms. She was very tired. Ebony jumped onto her lap, pretending to be a kitten again. 'It's just for a few months, Ebony. I have to look after Rewati until she's strong enough to go back to her mother, and the zoo. Then it'll be just you and me again.'

A few months . . . How long was a few months, Ebony thought without enthusiasm. He felt threatened by the new arrival. He watched every move, every feed, trying to read the signs with suspicion.

Two days after Rewati arrived at the Reeds', her blue eyes opened and she looked in bright astonishment at the world around her. On the thirteenth day, she took her first wobbling walk on cotton-wool legs. On the twenty-second day, she began to play, shaking her towel, making miniature growling noises.

Ebony watched the cub's progress with caution. He sensed that the oddly striped bundle of snowy fur was something special. So special that everyone endured the round-the-clock routine without grumbling. Elizabeth was worried by the huge responsibility. So many people enquired daily as to the infant tiger's progress. And she was the one who the cub depended upon for its life.

At first it was difficult to find a compatible feeding formula, but by varying the commercial product, they gradually found the right mixture for a baby tiger. Soon Rewati outgrew the incubator and graduated to a box. The rate of growth astonished Ebony. He sat, meticulously washing his face and grooming his whiskers, but watching all the time. It seemed that with every feed, Rewati grew an inch. She became a bouncing bundle of energy, full of mischief, lunging and rolling about like a puppy.

The big black tomcat took no notice of these antics, but he was disturbed when the tiger cub began crawling in tight circles on the floor making small noises and dragging her hind legs. Ebony sensed that something was very wrong and he wanted someone to come quickly. He began to miaow loudly. Elizabeth hurried in.

When the zoo's veterinary specialist arrived, Ebony moved away to a distance, but they did not seem to know what was the matter with the cub. They talked in low, worried voices. They tried antibiotics, oxygen treatments, outside exercise lessons and a formula pepped up with brandy and egg. Ebony's nose twitched at the smell. He wondered if he would be fed any of that delicious yellow stuff if he fell about on the floor.

But in a week the panic was over. Rewati recovered and was running around her garden jungle again. She graduated to baby cereal and strained beef in a bowl. Rewati was a sloppy eater, leaving most of it on her nose and face. Elizabeth always had a clean-up job with a damp washrag. Ebony helped too by licking out the bowl when no one was looking.

The jungle was a paradise of shrubs for hide and seek, camellia bushes on which to sharpen her claws and a big red ball for Rewati to pounce on and attack. She roamed free in the house, much to the surprise of visitors, unused to being greeted by a hefty playful tiger cub with formidable teeth and claws.

By now Rewati was trying to be friendly with Ebony. She wanted a playmate, but the black cat was having none of it. He'd seen those sharp claws puncture the red ball. He did not want to be similarly deflated.

Rewati chose her moment. She crept up to the unsuspecting Ebony and gave him a playful nuzzle in a soft spot. Ebony leaped into the air and up onto the fence. He sat there, totally outraged, licking down his disarranged fur. He glared down at the cub, whose baby blue eyes blinked back so innocently.

'Rewati needs someone to play with,' said Dr Reed.

Ebony could not believe his eyes when a second tiger cub arrived at the Reed household. The zoo had bought an orange Bengal cub as a playmate for Rewati. This cub was called Sakhi, which in Hindi means a close and dear companion.

Ebony was disgusted. He told Elizabeth in no uncertain terms. Now he had two half-wild creatures romping round his garden. He thought briefly about leaving home, but he loved Elizabeth too much. The yard had once been his domain; then it became a jungle for one baby to play in; now it was out-and-out tiger country. It became necessary to plot a course for safety with a dozen escape routes. He wasn't black and canny for nothing.

Rewati loved company. If she was left alone, she would howl and scratch and get into mischief. But if she could see someone, even just Ebony, she felt secure and happy.

As she grew bigger she was moved into new quarters in the basement. Elizabeth forgot to warn the man from the electric company about the new arrangement when he came to read the meter. He took quite a while to recover from the shock.

Rewati liked Elizabeth's company in the evening. The cub would curl up on the couch beside Elizabeth while they both watched television. Even the most boring programme took on a new lustre in such élite company, thought Elizabeth, stroking the white fur. She could rarely go out now. But when she did manage to get a brave tiger-sitting friend to stay for a while, the rule was: 'If the house catches fire, grab the cub first!'

The cub was now worth 35,000 dollars.

At two months old Rewati weighed a solid fifteen pounds and was eating ground beef. She greeted everyone in the Reed household with enthusiasm and affectionate chuffing noises. Ebony kept his distance. The young white tigress was already something of a handful. Friends were less keen on visiting. The cubs were becoming a rough and rowdy pair with teeth and claws that could hurt.

Ebony sensed something was different on that last day. Elizabeth was rather quiet. The two cubs were romping as usual in the garden and Ebony suddenly knew that they were going. He thought of all the friendly overtures he had dismissed. Perhaps he had been a little too stand-offish. His icy reserve melted a fraction at the thought of their imminent departure.

Crossing the yard, he stopped, eyeing a thrashing white-striped tiger tail. The temptation was too much. For a few moments he batted the tiger tail back and forth with his paw like the kitten he was at heart.

Rewati turned and looked over her shoulder, blue eyes wide with surprise. Was this a game two could play? Ebony straightened his back slowly, recovered his dignity and stalked off into the shrubs without a backward glance. He never saw Rewati again.

Two weeks later, Sakhi also returned to the zoo. The house very quiet and empty. Elizabeth wandered from room to room, at a loss without her tiger cubs. Ebony curled himself round her ankles. Remember me, he purred.

Elizabeth scooped him up into her arms, old friends, and nuzzled his dark head. 'They've gone. Just you and me now,' she said. '. . . until the next phone call.'

Rewati is never lonely now. She has all the company she wants: hundreds of thousands of children visit the zoo every year to admire the magnificent fully grown white tigress.

Life returned to normal for Ebony. His patience was rewarded and he regained his rightful place in the Reed household.

He no longer shares Elizabeth's lap with a frisky white tiger cub. The garden is his, and the vacuum cleaner. Peace has returned.

The Uninvited Guest

It was not long after we moved into our house that I saw the black cat walk into the larder. The occurrence was unusual as we did not have a cat. I thought perhaps a neighbour's pet had come to inspect the newcomers.

I could see him quite clearly from the corner of my eye . . . a large handsome black cat with long curving tail and alert pointed ears.

For a moment I paused, not wanting to scare him. Then I went over to say hello.

There was nothing. Empty air. The larder was stacked with tidy rows of bottles, jars and tins, the bread bin, vegetable rack . . . but no cat. I searched the larder thoroughly but he had completely disappeared.

Puzzled, I shut the door. We had made the larder from a large walk-in cupboard under the stairs. It was ideal; cool and ventilated and a blissful size after our cramped years in rented accommodation. Everything about the house was a long-awaited dream come true. It was old, weather-beaten red brick, brimming with character and space, with a rambling garden made for children and animals. We had the children, two daughters, Linda and Janice, and I had promised them a cat and a dog as soon as we settled in.

I began to search the house. I had clearly seen that cat, and yet there was no cat. Odd.

'What are you doing, Mummy?' asked my eight-year-old curiously, as I peered under beds.

'Er . . . just checking,' I said.

'Checking for what?' she persisted.

'Dust,' I said.

I sat back on my heels, pushing the hair off my face. I must be tired, I thought. The move had been hectic and there was still such a lot to do, getting the house straight and redecorated as well as caring for the family. Perhaps it had been a shadow, a very dark shadow.

It was easy enough to tell myself this, but I didn't believe it, not for one moment. I know a cat when I see one.

'Mummy, isn't it nearly tea-time?'

I shrugged off the incident and returned to the world of tea, baths and bedtime stories, dismissing the cat from my mind. What did it matter anyway? It had obviously found a way out of the house.

That same evening as I stood in the kitchen making a late drink, I saw the cat again. He was sitting on the floor near the larder, looking straight at me. There was no mistaking him this time . . . a big black cat with his tail curled neatly over his paws.

'Hello, puss,' I said. 'Where have you come from?'

I was talking to myself. It was ridiculous, but there was nothing there. The cat had completely vanished. I made a brief search of the kitchen but there was no way he could have got out.

'I just don't understand it,' I said to my husband, Neville, as I went back into the living room with our two mugs of hot chocolate. 'I saw a black cat in the kitchen this afternoon. It went into the larder. Then just now I saw the same cat, sitting outside the larder.'

'So? You've seen a black cat. By the larder. Perhaps he's hungry.'

I shook my head. 'No, it vanished into thin air. That's

what's so strange,' I said. 'It was definitely there, and then it wasn't.'

'You're imagining things,' said Neville.

'Once perhaps, but not twice,' I said firmly.

As the weeks went by I saw the cat almost daily, but only in the kitchen, either disappearing into the larder or sitting near it. I often spoke to him softly, but soon learned that if I made any movement towards him the cat vanished instantly.

'Puss, puss,' I said coaxingly. 'Come and talk to me. I won't hurt you.'

The cat stared at me, his slanting amber eyes unblinking, thinking secret thoughts in a secret world. His coat was a furry blackness that I longed to touch, to feel its softness.

'Talking to yourself again?' said Neville, grinning.

'I was talking to the cat,' I said. 'Are you sure you didn't see it?'

'No. Nothing. Not a black cat in sight.'

Everything about the kitchen was so normal. The warmth, the delicious smell of a casserole cooking, sunshine streaming through the window, curtains moving with the fresh breeze. We were not far from the sea. It was all quite ordinary. There was no icy chill, no hush, no premonition . . . only a mysterious cat that came and went like a ghost.

I made some enquiries. There was no large black cat living in the neighbourhood; the previous occupants of our house had not owned a cat.

Linda and Janice knew nothing about the uninvited guest in our house. I did not want to frighten them, although they occasionally caught me talking to thin air.

'Mummy,' one of them would giggle. 'You're talking to yourself again!'

I was sure that the cat could see me. It had a definite expression in its eyes as it stared across the kitchen. There was nothing unseeing about those eyes. I could not describe the look. I tried to find the words . . . the cat looked contented, almost serene.

It was some seven months later, a warm day in early summer, when my daughter Linda called from the kitchen, her voice high with excitement.

'Mummy, Mummy, there's a black cat just gone in the larder! A big black cat. Is it ours? Can we keep it?'

The girls had been wanting a cat for ages and I had promised them a cat and a dog. There just hadn't been time to look for the right pets.

'Oh, really?' I said, going into the kitchen. 'I bet you can't find him in there now.'

Linda looked inside the cupboard under the stairs, clattering around, but she came out mystified, her innocent face looking puzzled.

'But he's not there,' she said. 'How funny. I saw him go in.'

'I often see this cat,' I said casually, as if I were talking about some mundane daily routine. 'But he's not an ordinary cat. He can disappear, just like that.'

The child laughed at my impersonation of Tommy Cooper.

'You mean a ghost cat?'

I nodded. 'I think so, but there's no need to be frightened of him. He means no harm. He's quite friendly in a remote sort of way.'

Linda did not seem in the least alarmed. She quite liked the idea of having a ghost cat. 'We'll call him Spooky,' she said.

Linda only saw Spooky occasionally, but I saw him often. I got quite used to the black cat sitting by the larder or walking into it. I began to wonder if the cupboard under the stairs had been used as an air-raid shelter during the war years and he was waiting to take cover; or perhaps his favourite sleeping place had been in some dark recess under the stairs. I felt sure he must have lived in the house at some time.

'Hello, Spooky,' I said, standing quite still and returning his gaze. Cat and I stared at each other. It was a strange sensation, knowing that when I moved, the cat would instantly disappear.

We had not mentioned Spooky to Janice, my six-year-old daughter. We thought she was a little too young to cope with such an unusual phenomenon, even a friendly furry one.

One evening in August, we were downstairs watching television. I was knitting and thinking about the new baby I was expecting soon. Suddenly we heard Janice calling from her bed.

'Mummy! Mummy! Mummy!'

I raced upstairs as quickly as my size would allow and rushed into her bedroom. She was sitting up in bed, her eyes wide with fright.

'Mummy, Mummy, there's a big cat on my bed,' she cried. 'Take him off, take him off. He jumped on me and frightened me.'

'Is he still there? Where?' I asked, for I could see nothing.

'Yes,' she said, calming down but still trembling a little. 'He's leaning on my legs. He's ever so heavy.'

She was obviously getting over the fright, for she put out her hand and began stroking the cat. I was amazed to see her hand making the movement of actually stroking a non-existent cat. It was to be the only time anyone actually touched or felt the black cat. And I was not surprised that it was Janice who was given this gift. For she was and still is quite mad about cats.

I almost expected to hear a purr as Janice stroked the air, but there was nothing except my daughter's cooing and coaxing voice, then the rustle of bed sheets as I tucked her back to bed. Outside the house, the summer breeze combed the long grass and whispered to the nodding leaves.

'Spooky,' I said quite firmly. 'You are not to go waking the children when they are asleep and frightening them.'

I think he must have heard me, for Spooky was never again seen upstairs. Perhaps Janice's first reaction had alarmed him. He returned to his old haunts in the kitchen and all three of us saw him often. But never my husband.

A year after we moved in, our son Bradley arrived and about the same time we got a cat of our own. She was the runt of a litter and not expected to survive, but with some hand-feeding and lots of care, she grew into a lovely little black cat with white nose and paws. We called her Snagglepuss, after the tatty old cartoon lion.

One day the girls were playing in the field opposite the house where there were some ruined farmbuildings waiting for demolition, when they found the remains of a black cat. It appeared to have been squashed flat by some old machinery, although that may just have been the appearance it gave after decomposition.

The girls were very upset and wanted to give the cat a proper funeral. They dug a little hole and buried it wrapped in silver foil like a spacesuit, shed tears and said a little prayer.

'Maybe this was our Spooky,' I said, picking some wild flowers to put on the little grave. 'Perhaps he's at peace now and won't visit us again.'

He did, but less frequently. The family were growing up and when Linda left school and began working, she brought home a stray kitten, a pretty little tabby female which we immediately adopted and called Twinkletoes, Twinks for short. Perhaps Spooky was beginning to feel crowded out in our household, for Brad was a normal, noisy eight-year-old and we also had a red setter called Crackers, short for Meadway Caractacus.

Twinks settled down with Snagglepuss and Crackers and she grew into a beautiful cat with gentle, loving ways. Spooky was part of our family too, but only females saw him, human females – or so we thought.

Brad was fifteen and getting ready for bed one night. He was on his own in the house as we were out. Suddenly he heard the most terrible racket coming from the

43

kitchen. He hurried downstairs and on opening the door was nearly knocked flat by Twinks, who leaped out, eyes wild and staring, her black striped fur standing on end.

She flew upstairs into his bedroom and hid under the chest of drawers. She refused to come out, her eyes transfixed with fright.

Brad searched the kitchen but could find nothing amiss. Puzzled, he went back to bed, Twinks still crouched in the furthermost corner under the chest of drawers.

'Mum,' he said the next morning. 'You should have seen Twinks last night. It's a wonder you didn't hear her! There was a terrible commotion in the kitchen. What a racket! I went down and Twinks shot out of the kitchen and up the stairs, breaking the sound barrier, I bet. She got under my chest of drawers and refused to come out. I wonder what on earth got into her?'

Twinks was sitting on the landing, peering down the stairs through the bannisters. She looked most unhappy. I took it that she needed to go out, having been indoors all night.

'Come on, Twinks,' I said encouragingly. 'Out into the garden.'

She did not move. I didn't have time for playing games so I went upstairs and picked her up to take outside. As I reached the hall, Twinks stiffened in my arms. I went towards the kitchen, intending to open the back door. It was too much for Twinks. With a screech, she leaped out of my arms and raced upstairs again. There was no way that cat was going into the kitchen. She was obviously terrified.

'For heaven's sake, Twinks,' I said. 'What's the matter with you?'

But I had a shrewd idea. Twinks had met Spooky.

I eventually got her out of the front door. From then on she refused to go into the kitchen. She avoided all contact with the floor, using every available piece of furniture to walk on. She insisted on being carried to bed by Brad. Her eyes always had a staring, frightened look and any slight movement or noise sent her into a panic with her fur standing on end.

During these months Spooky was never seen. Perhaps Twinks' reaction had alarmed him too. Twinks is a very pretty female cat and it could be he longed for some cat company.

Twinks has slowly recovered but still leaps off the floor as if it is hot coals. She sometimes ventures a little way into the kitchen. The encounter – or whatever it was – has changed her. She is extremely nervous.

Now Spooky seems to have gone forever and I often wonder if it was the presence of the girls in the house that brought him to us. Perhaps he once belonged to a little girl in the past.

Laura, our two-year-old grand-daughter often comes to visit us. She's a sweet little girl with long fair hair and big brown eyes. She loves pets and shows no fear, playing with Twinks for hours.

I was sitting in the living room, sewing, the sun streaming in through the window. We have half a dozen finches now and are hoping to build an aviary in the garden. Twinks is sunning herself in a warm spot.

Laura is wandering about, going into the kitchen to fetch some toys left on the floor.

'Nice pussy,' I hear her say. 'Nice pussy . . .'

I keep quite still, listening. I wonder if I am imagining things. But no, her childlike voice is cooing and coaxing something.

'Puss, puss, puss . . .' she is saying.

Perhaps she is playing with her toys, or talking to Twinks through the window. Perhaps our strange visitor is back. Maybe one day she will ask me about a big black cat sitting by the larder.

Lucky's Story

She sat on the roof of a lorry sunning herself. She liked sitting up high, looking over the world, out of the way of the traffic, pedestrians and hotel guests.

Not that she had anything against hotel guests. They were part of her life and made a fuss of her. But there were so many of them and they were always changing.

These people were on something called a holiday. But since they ate, drank, talked and slept in much the same way as on ordinary days, Lucky could not see the difference.

Lucky dozed in the sunshine, dreaming dreams, chasing fleeing thoughts of other places that must be somewhere. She knew the world was a large place; that there were streets beyond this street, perhaps even a town beyond this town. It was all there waiting to be explored.

'One day you'll be carried away,' said the woman, lifting Lucky down from the cab roof. 'You have been warned.'

Lucky put her claws into the woman's short and shining black hair that hung like silk on each side of her face. Lucky called the woman Lindiladi. She liked her a lot. It was a mutual feeling.

'Come on, you soft thing,' said Lindiladi, carrying the cat indoors. 'I've enough to do without having to keep looking for you.'

Lucky was nine months old, having grown from an adorable white kitten with a black tail into a big and elegant cat with thick white fur and piercing green eyes. The top of her head was also black, and looked like a superior Frank Sinatra hair-piece. She had three pink pads on her paws and one black.

She was an affectionate cat. She knew that Lindiladi had rescued her from the RSPCA kennels, where animals disappeared if they were not claimed. But she was also very independent. Lucky had her own ideas about a lot of things, as did Lindiladi. That's why they got on so well. Lucky often jumped onto Lindiladi's knee and put her small nose right up to the woman's nose.

'You must have Eskimo blood,' said Lindiladi, amused, stroking the thick white fur.

Lucky did not understand about Eskimos but she liked to hear Lindiladi's soft laugh. The young woman was always working, so was her husband, whom Lucky called Peterman. Having a hotel meant a lot of work and no time to sit on the top of lorries, decided Lucky, as she escaped again into the fresh sea air. She stopped and sniffed; the pungent ozone was tantalisingly full of the smell of fish and seabirds and great oceans. Inland she sensed the mountains of the Lake District. She had not seen an ocean nor a mountain and she wondered why she knew these things.

It was Sunday, 21 April 1981, though Lucky did not know the date. Lindiladi put Lucky out on the doorstep. A scurry of wind whipped the woman's short hair against her face, and ruffled the cat's white fur like a flurry of snow.

'Now please be good,' said Lindiladi. 'I'm going to have a very busy day and I haven't time to waste hunting for you. Just stay around here.'

Lucky arched her back and swished her long black tail

and tipped the end over into a raised question mark. Of course she would be good. She was happy to oblige. It was too windy to go exploring. She would just take a look around the warehouse and see what was going on.

Near to the hotel was an antique dealer's shop and warehouse. Lucky considered this one of her favourite places to play. It had a particular smell all of its own, of houses long ago shut up and deserted, of cats and dogs and mice from the past. She sniffed at the clinging aromas of cigars and beeswax, dust and decay . . . it was all so interesting.

The owner did not seem to mind if Lucky padded around inspecting things. There was a cabinet-maker who was kind and gave her an occasional saucer of milk, but he was busy.

Lucky prowled around the antique furniture: Victorian tables and button-back tête-à-tête chairs; old pictures in heavy frames with cracked varnish; pots and bowls and old china. She liked all the different woods: rosewood, fruitwood, walnut, and ancient oak, knotted with veins of dried sap.

There was a lot of activity in the yard for a Sunday. They were packing a large container for delivery somewhere. Lucky danced across the yard chasing a woodshaving, pouncing on it as it caught against a railing. This was going to be a fun day.

It was late that night when Lindiladi finally finished work and went outside to call in Lucky.

'Lucky-lucky-lucky.' It was the familiar call sign. The woman peered into the darkness. No white ghost emerged sideways from the shadows, casual and off-hand as if just passing by.

'Lucky-lucky-lucky.'

Lindiladi was getting worried. Lucky always came when she was called. There was such a lot of traffic in Morecambe, and Lucky was only just past kittenhood. She did not have all her road-sense yet.

'I can't find Lucky,' said Lindiladi.

'Probably having a night out,' said Peterman. 'Don't worry, she'll be back in the morning.'

But she wasn't. Lindiladi was up and out early before her duties at the hotel got into swing. She searched the streets and gardens, and then went across to the warehouse. She knew Lucky played there sometimes. It was 8 a.m. A large container stood in the yard, sealed and ready for collection.

'Have you seen my cat?' she asked the men. 'It's a white cat with black on its head and a black tail.'

They shook their heads. 'No, sorry . . .'

Lucky heard Lindiladi's voice, so she knew her beloved mistress was not far away. This was reassuring. The woman always found her. She would this time, too. Lucky yawned. This place was airless and making her drowsy. She had had a lovely time playing among the furniture, but now she was tired. She found some brown paper that was warm and just asking to be trampled into a bed.

A sudden jolt brought her sharply out of her sleep. Something very strange was happening.

The world was being tilted. There were harsh, unrecognisable noises. Bolts clanged. Then an engine was switched on. Lucky was confused . . . was she sitting on top of a lorry? Was this the moment to jump off into Lindiladi's arms?

But she couldn't jump. It was dark, and the darkness was full of shapes. There was no room to move. Lucky uncurled herself and miaowed loudly, but the engine revs drowned her call. A first tremor of fear ran along her spine, a prickle of alarm. This was all quite new and she was unsure how to react. She knew Lindiladi would be along for her soon. She miaowed again as she felt the movement growing within the darkness and the rattling and jolting throwing her from side to side.

Lucky crouched in her small place; two piercing green eyes searching for a solution. If only she could understand what was happening, then perhaps she could do something.

She tried to sleep again, but was unable to settle because of a growing thirst; then hunger. She prowled, squeezing herself small, sniffing and exploring. There was nothing. Pangs contracted her stomach and she miaowed helplessly, but no one heard.

Life was no longer the Morecambe sunshine and the smell of the sea in the air; it was a dark nightmare of unexpected jolts and endless vibration. Suddenly that movement stopped and, after a pause, a new sensation of swinging took its place. Lucky was thrown from her weak precarious balance, sickened as she lurched into the air; she heard the grinding and grunting of machinery: a throbbing, deafening power that grew into a crescendo of noise.

Lucky was terrified. She was convinced she was about to be devoured by some huge monster with gaping jaws. But it did not happen.

She was tortured by hunger and thirst. She sniffed dust, chewed paper, wood. Her limbs were racked with pain. Then as she lay, weak and exhausted, waiting to die, a trickle of condensation ran down the metal walls and her small tongue licked at the moisture as if it were nectar.

She followed the trickles everywhere, wiping them clean, licking and licking until her tongue was sore against the metal. But it came again, the life-saving water, replaced by some miracle that she did not question.

She was beyond all thought. Home had faded from her mind like a sweet, almost-forgotten dream. That was all so long ago, misty and unreal. Time meant nothing, stretching into a long dark tunnel of misery. She became weaker and weaker, life ebbing from her bright eyes.

But she clung to some intangible thread. She dragged herself to the trickles of moisture, her once-soft mouth now dry and cracked. A tiny flame of spirit still flickered in her heart, but it had almost gone out.

She could hardly stir herself any more. She was drifting into unconsciousness, but then somewhere it registered in her mind that all was quite still. The endless movement had stopped. She could almost hear the stillness and the silence. Perhaps this was death. Perhaps she had died.

Light streamed against her closed eyes. It blinded her. Yes, this was death.

Lucky hovered in the twilight zone between life and death. She was not aware of the strange voices, the rough but gentle hands that lifted her, the exclamations of astonishment.

'Hell. A dead cat!'

'Are you sure it's dead?'

'Yeah . . . chuck it away. Poor thing. Must have starved to death.'

'Let me look at it. I think it's still breathing very faintly.'

'Aw, leave it alone. It's a goner, Gary. We've got enough to do.'

'I'm taking it to the veterinary surgeon. It deserves a chance. It must have been in that damned container near on nine weeks.'

In the days that followed Lucky knew very little of what was happening to her, and she certainly knew nothing of the frantic searching and newspaper advertisements as Lindiladi combed the streets and pubs of Morecambe for her cat.

Lucky found herself in an amazing place. Everything smelt quite different; everything was so big. As she looked around her for the first time, it was as if an explosion had taken place and the outside of everything had disappeared, blown away. Where was she? And where was Lindiladi?

In her confusion she slipped in and out of consciousness, but gained on each encounter with this new world. She was drip-fed, injected, massaged, cared for as if she was worth a thousand dollars.

Her first sip of milk was an unforgettable moment. She almost fell out of the man's arms in her ecstasy. It tasted different, but it was milk all the same.

'Hold on,' laughed the man, Gary Fingleman. 'Not so fast. It won't go away, and there's lots more.'

When Lucky was strong enough, he no longer had to feed her by bottle. In three weeks she was able to stand and sip from a saucer. This new place had lovely food. Lucky ate well and sat in the blazing sunshine, dozing in the heat. She spent her convalescence with the man she called Fingleman. Sometimes she sat on his knee and purred, but he was still a stranger.

Lucky had always thought there must be somewhere beyond Morecambe, and perhaps this was it. People spoke differently; the cars and lorries were hugely terrifying; Fingleman had a refrigerator the size of a small room.

She liked the climate, but she missed the birds. And she missed Lindiladi. Sometimes she asked Fingleman where her beloved mistress was, but he did not understand and would just scratch behind her ear and grin, and pour her some milk from a carton.

It was August and almost unbearably hot. Lucky sat on the man's lap while he drank a cold beer. The telephone rang.

'Is that Gary Fingleman of Houston, Texas?' asked a woman. 'I know this sounds very strange, but I think you've got my cat.'

'Oh?' he drawled. 'Why should you think I've got your cat?'

'Last April I lost my cat Lucky. She just disappeared. I've just met a man who works in the antique shop opposite where we used to live, and he said an American came into the shop to buy some more antiques and said thanks for the extra package. There was a cat in his last delivery, half-dead. A big black and white cat with a black tail . . .' Lindiladi got the words out in one big rush.

'Sealand's sitting on my knee now,' said Fingleman, stroking Lucky's head. 'But how do I know she's your cat?'

'Look under her paws. She has three pink pads, but her right paw pad is black.'

Lucky suddenly found herself upended on Fingleman's lap, her paws waving in the air. He grasped them gently but firmly. She wriggled frantically. Her paws were very ticklish.

'Three pink paws and one black. Then this must be your Lucky, and lucky she is to have survived the journey to Houston. Four thousand and five hundred miles, lady.'

Lucky did not hear Lindiladi weeping at the other end of the telephone, but she knew something was happening. Her fur crept and she ran under a table, nightmare memories of the container sweeping back.

'She was just bones when I found her, but she's putting on a little weight now.'

'But how on earth do I get her home from America?' Lindiladi asked, dazed.

'We'll see she goes home in style,' said Fingleman, knowing that he must let the cat go.

It was the media that got Lucky home. She had taken herself to America, but it was the combined forces of newspapers, television, local radio and British Caledonian who reunited Lindiladi and Lucky.

While Lucky grew stronger in the Texas sunshine, the wheels went round, forms were filled in, people wrote things, took her photograph.

She was used to the veterinary surgeon and his needles, and she thought no more than a fractional irritation when yet one more injection went into her flesh. Fingleman was holding her in a firm grasp, and looking at her with a strange, fond look. The last thing she saw before sleep overtook her was his kind, strong face.

53

She knew nothing of the transfer to Houston airport or the long flight. Her limbs twitched in a deep slumber; dreams tumbled through her mind: the wild, wet rain and the smell of the sea . . . the dry baking heat of the past few weeks . . . the terror of the remembrance of that other place, small, dark, endlessly jolting her towards death.

Someone was carrying her into a small room. Lucky yawned. She was dry and sleepy, barely awake, her mouth like sawdust. With a tremendous effort she opened one eye . . . Lindiladi was coming into the room with another young woman holding her arm.

'Lucky . . . Lucky . . . my darling Lucky.' Lindiladi held her for a few brief moments, tears pouring down her cheeks. Of course it was her Lucky, a very thin and skinny Lucky, but still her beautiful cat.

Lucky tried to purr, but sleep overcame her, washing her back into dreams. Her last thought was where had Lindiladi been all this time? It was all . . . yawn . . . very strange.

At the quarantine kennels in Blackpool Lucky had her first English press conference. A lot of people looking at her and expecting something.

'How do you know it's your cat?' snapped the reporters. 'How can you be sure?'

Lindiladi was asked the same thing over and over again, even though she had brought photographs taken of Lucky before she went to America.

'You can see it's her,' said Lindiladi. 'Look, the same black tail, the black head, one black paw pad.'

A man came into the back of the room, unseen.

'Lucky-lucky-lucky,' he called.

Lucky looked up instantly and turned her head towards the voice. It was an echo from the past. Her call-sign. It broke through the long nightmare and the unreal days that had followed in that foreign land. It brought back sunning on top of lorries, the hotel guests, the antique shop. She made as if to spring towards

Peterman, a cry of freedom caught in her throat as she thought again of smelling the ozone and hearing the shrieks of the seabirds.

'You see . . .' said Lindiladi triumphantly. 'She *is* my Lucky. That's proof.'

Lucky waited out the long, boring six months' quarantine with commendable patience, reassured because Lindiladi came to see her every weekend. Lindiladi brought tinned salmon and cartons of cream, which Lucky ate because they were gifts of love and not because she was hungry.

They grew to know each other again, and one day Lucky jumped onto the woman's lap and put a small pink nose up to touch Lindiladi's nose.

'My little Eskimo,' said the woman.

Nearly a year passed before Lucky at long last returned home. She found that they now all lived in a shop. She took the new changes very quietly, sitting sometimes with a remoteness that was impenetrable.

At first Lucky would only sleep on Lindiladi's bed. The nightmares came often and her body shook. Then she would wake suddenly, sit up and look around at the sleeping figure and the dark hair on the pillow, reassuring herself that she was home; she was safe.

Sometimes Lucky gnawed thoughtfully on a piece of wood, the taste of timber still lingering in her mouth. She did not wander far. She had done her travelling.

Then, amid great activity, the shop was sold and another hotel bought. A popular feature of the new hotel is Lucky's bar.

Lucky sits on the bar counter, Persil white, poised and elegant, her press cuttings and photographs on the wall behind her. She wonders about all the fuss. Why people want to have their photograph taken with the cat who went to America on her own. Anyone knows it's just the next place on.

Churchill's Cats

Jock II sat at the foot of the stairs patiently waiting for the doors to open. It was then that the visitors would begin to arrive. He did not know why there were often so many people about, but few failed to give him a friendly pat.

At other times the Elizabethan manor house was empty and Jock II padded silently through the deserted rooms like another of its many ghosts. He saw nothing but he sensed them. The vibrations were frequently so strong that Jock would perk an ear, his whiskers twitching, alert for the merest whisper from the past.

'What a cute cat! Isn't he cute? My goodness, and did you say Winston Churchill had a cat just like this one?' enthused the American woman, eyes bright with curiosity for every detail of the great man.

'Exactly like this one, a beautiful marmalade cat. Jock was Mr Churchill's favourite cat,' said the guide. 'And they always fed him just here in the kitchen.'

'You don't say? Fancy that. Can we see Jock being fed? You know, like it was the same cat?'

Jock II moved into position. This was what he had been waiting for. He was programmed for it. The visitors, especially the Americans, loved seeing him being fed. Obediently he ate his breakfast from a dish put on the same spot as his predecessor's dish. He re-enacted the past with enthusiasm for a spellbound audience.

Time had stopped still in the house; the library, drawing and dining rooms, and the study were left exactly as they had been in October 1964.

Jock wandered out into the garden and sat on the paving stones to wash his face. It was a large garden, sweeping down to a small valley and rising to a wooded ridge. The sun glinted serenely on the surface of the lake, barely disturbing the ducks and swans that glided between the rushes.

Jock II knew he had been chosen because of his resemblance to Jock I. It gave him the strangest feeling as if he were acting in a play, taking the part of this earlier cat, acting out a previous life.

He did not know this other Jock, had never met him. He knew there had been lots of cats . . . Nelson, Smoky, Gabrielle, Tango . . . he had heard them spoken of many times. The great man had loved cats.

Jock II yawned delicately in the dappled sunlight and stretched himself. The visitors milled about the garden, admiring the views, the rose gardens that had been planted for Clementine, the ornamental pools, the brick walls. The other cats came and gathered around him silently, contemplating his sleeping marmalade form.

'I was here when he built that wall,' said the tabby at last. 'I used to sit and watch him. Slap, slap. He really liked bricklaying. It was a way of relaxing. Slap, slap. And he was good at it. He could lay a brick a minute. He used to tell me about wars in many distant places as he took a trowelful of cement and slapped it on a brick. Slap, slap. I think I was his favourite cat. You could say I helped him build that wall.'

'I knew him during a war,' said Nelson, a short-haired black cat. 'I lived in the war rooms in London. A marine gave me to him. He was very pleased. It was pretty spooky living underground. Everything was grey or khaki, and tin hats and gas masks lined the walls. I did my bit for the war effort; I caught mice down there. I was only allowed out when the all-clear sounded, then I'd race across the road to St James's Park to chase the ducks!'

The cats yawned, scratched, and changed places by leaping over the slumbering cat.

'He had me evacuated,' Nelson went on. 'Perhaps I was his favourite . . .'

'Evacuated? Evacuated? What does that mean?'

'It was during the height of the blitz. Those sirens used to make my fur stand on end. There was a very bad raid one night; he got all the staff into the shelters. A bomb dropped and the kitchen of Number Ten was extensively damaged, so he had me sent into the country, where it was safer. I was evacuated to Chequers. He knew I was very frightened with all the explosions and bombs dropping. But it meant I didn't see him so often. He could only come some weekends and then I would sit on his knee and let him stroke me. He was very busy with the war.'

A beautiful long-haired black Persian sniffed and swished her tail imperiously. 'Poof . . . I was in the secret Cabinet war rooms in Whitehall too. I didn't let people stroke me! Oh no, except perhaps one lady who let me sit on her desk. I bit people. I laddered stockings – and they were very precious in the war, you know. You could say I was unpopular, but it didn't bother me. I had my own war going. But he liked me; he liked a cat with spirit.' Smoky sniffed again, her eyes gleaming with memories of the mischief she had got up to among all those telephones and maps and charts.

'But I don't think I ever bit him,' she growled knowingly.

The cats fell silent, thinking of the man in his siren suit, his fat cigar that puffed smoke into their eyes, the big coat with the astrakhan collar. They were unaware of another group of cats coming to join them. They approached unheralded, hesitant, wary, ears flattened . . .

There was one cat, half wild, not sure how to

communicate with these sophisticated, cosseted and domesticated felines. He dodged and danced about a little, remembering how he had to escape the hooves of horses trotting on the cobblestones.

'He was six years old when he made friends with me,' he said at last. 'I lived in the stables at Blenheim Palace and he was always there looking at the horses. I remember one day in April we were playing in the grounds. We were playing wars. He had been building encampments and pitched an umbrella for a tent. I didn't understand the game but it was great fun and the umbrella kept rolling about in the wind. I know I was not his favourite cat, but I may have been his first.'

A pair of thin grey tabbies twisted themselves around each other, grinning wickedly, ears pricked with enjoyment.

'Oh brother, he liked horses all right. He was fourteen when he and his brother Jack came to Banstead Manor, near Newmarket, for a holiday. They both went straight down to the stables, even though there was four inches of snow. He didn't know there were two of us, and we played such tricks on him!'

'Leaping out.'

'Rushing round corners.'

'Climbing over stalls.'

'When he discovered there were two of us, he laughed and laughed. It was a good trick.'

'And he had a good holiday, shooting rabbits and rats and skating on the pond.'

The cat from Cairo sat apart, pale and dignified. He had lived in the barracks of the 21st Lancers. The cavalry charge at the battle of Omdurman on 2 September 1898 had been a dreadful, gory day. Many of the cat's soldier friends did not come back, but one special young friend returned, weary, battle-stained, but triumphant.

'I was under fire all day and rode through the charge,' the man wrote to his mother by candlelight. 'Nothing touched me.'

The cat kept him company as he began to write his second book, an account of the whole Sudan campaign called *The River War*. He wrote all day, every day, and far into the night till his hands were seized by cramp. He would rub the pain out of his fingers, stroke the cat's soft fur, then go back to his writing.

The cat from Cairo wondered whether to tell the others these things and how well he knew the man as a young fearless soldier, but he did not think they would understand. It was all such a long time ago. So he said nothing.

Out of the shadows slunk a timid greyish-brown creature. It was half-starved, with ribs sticking out. Yet something kept its valiant spirit burning.

'He hated every minute of being imprisoned,' the cat hissed as he crawled along the ground. 'It was in Pretoria in 1899. He was caught by the Boers after an armoured train ambush. The prison was an awful place. He tried to make friends with me to take his mind off being a prisoner. I tried to catch the vermin but I was so weak. He gave me some of his food. I'll never forget that. When he escaped over the prison wall, I lost my friend. I cried for days and days.'

The other cats looked uncomfortable. They did not know anything about prisons and ambushes. It was out of their experience.

'He was never my friend,' howled a feral cat from Venice. 'I spat and hissed at him. But he only had eyes for his young wife as they glided past the palazzos in a gondola. He was on his honeymoon and they looked so round and happy, whereas we were starving and miserable, roaming the alleyways and bridges. What could I do but hiss? He didn't hear.'

Jock II stirred in his sleep as if a cold wind had blown through his fur, ruffling the russet layers on his back. His paws twitched in combat with some dream adversary, neither losing nor winning.

Gabrielle detached herself from the group, an elegant

cream and brown Siamese with slanting blue eyes. She surveyed the gathering with a haughty disdain.

'It was none of you. I was his favourite, of course. I was her cat, their pet. I didn't have to work for my living, or steal or fight. Pedigree cats don't work. My life was one of luxury and ease. I'm sure he had the fishpond put in just for me.'

'You were the destructive one,' said Tango, a long-tailed tangerine-coloured cat with amber eyes full of wisdom. 'You were the one that clawed the Coronation chairs.'

'I did not,' Gabrielle denied huffily.

'The claw marks are still there,' said Tango.

'He wrote home sending tender love to Clemmie and his little kittens, and he thought the Prince of Wales should fall in love with a pretty cat,' said Gabrielle, preening herself.

'He didn't mean you,' said Tango. 'He sometimes called his children the kittens, and his concern for the young future king is beyond your comprehension. He thought that young man too thin and too spartan.'

'You were jealous of my position in the house-hold.' Gabrielle arched her back. 'Just because you are in a silly painting. Who'd want to be in a painting? I couldn't be bothered to keep still. No one could paint my unique colouring.'

'Sir William Nicholson put me in the painting because I didn't mind posing,' said Tango. 'I just curled up and went to sleep. It was their Silver Wedding picture so I knew it was something very special. Perhaps that makes me their favourite cat,' he added, knowing it would annoy Gabrielle.

'It certainly does not,' said Gabrielle, reacting furiously. 'You look like a bowl of fruit in that painting. You look like a bowl of oranges.'

Tango did not bother to argue with her. It did not worry him what Gabrielle said. He curled himself into a comfortable position and went back to sleep. He knew

61

only too well how much he had been loved by the master.

'Tango? Tango . . .' he could hear the gruff voice calling him now. If only he knew where to go, he would follow. They had always been so happy together, had such fun. There was no need to wonder about favourites. It did not matter.

'But what about me?' asked a pert little tabby. 'After all, I was the only one he advertised for. He actually put a card in the window for me.'

'Heaven preserve us,' groaned Gabrielle. 'We've all heard this a dozen times before. Do we have to hear it again?'

'Yes, you do,' the tabby insisted. 'It's my story and it's a good story. I had been, well . . . a little naughty – '

'Very naughty,' Tango yawned.

'And I was put out—'

'After a good hard slap with a rolled-up newspaper,' said Gabrielle.

'So I ran away. Any self-respecting cat would run away after being slapped with a rolled-up newspaper. Sarah was seventeen then and she told her father that I had run away. He was very worried about me and he told his secretary that if she wished she could put a card in the widow saying: "IF CAT CARES TO COME HOME, ALL IS FORGIVEN." He said it in fun, of course, but wasn't it nice that he should think of me?'

The tabby pranced around, still hugely amused by the whole idea. But then other memories returned and her dancing stopped.

'And did you go back?' asked one of the strange foreign cats who had not heard the story before.

'Not until ten days later. They searched and searched everywhere for me. They found me with a snare round my neck. It was horrible. Everyone was so upset.'

An uneasiness fell upon the group of cats. They all knew about snares and traps and the cruel things that could happen to an unwary cat, even to a cat from the best of circumstances.

'But you were found and rescued,' said a magnificent marmalade cat, speaking for the first time. 'Think how lucky you were. He really liked cats. And he liked some dogs. Monty's two dogs, Rommel and Hitler, were friendly little things, despite their names. And remember how he drew sketches of little cats and pigs at the end of his letters to Clementine to amuse her?'

'Those pigs!'

'Pigs . . . urgh,' the cats chorused. 'How could he?'

'And his special name for her was Cat, not always Clemmie.'

Jock II nearly awoke with a start. He stared at the newcomer. He was seeing a mirror image of himself. A big marmalade cat with the same markings and proud head. It was uncanny. Surely this must be the original Jock, the most famous cat of all.

'I must have spent more time with him than the rest of you put together,' mused the first Jock. 'He had always been so busy with travelling and wars. But he was getting old and I used to sit on his knee in his wheelchair and they would wheel us around the gardens together. He slept a lot and I was allowed to stay on his bed. I knew he took comfort from me, for often in his sleep his hand would stray to my head and he would stroke me gently. I was with him, right to the very end.'

A hush fell like a shroud upon the cats. They stayed still and silent. Only Gabrielle arched her back and lashed her rope of a tail.

'I don't believe you,' she spat.

'Does it really matter whether you believe it,' said Tango wisely. 'Does it matter who was actually there, as long as someone was with him?'

'And I should know, shouldn't I?' Jock sighed. 'It was such a long time ago. And I grieved for him. I was sad for weeks and weeks, looking for him everywhere.'

Up the long sweep of the lawn a small black cat came

scampering with a rolling gait as if the earth was moving beneath his paws.

'Am I too late? Do you remember me?' he panted. 'I had my photograph taken with him for the newpapers! He was on board the Navy ship, the *Prince of Wales*, to meet President Roosevelt. It was in August 1941, during the Second World War. They had their photographs taken for all the newspapers; then as they were moving across the deck together, he stopped to stroke me. He had seen me among all those important people! A photographer snapped the shot. Me, the ship's cat! I was famous, too. A lucky black cat, he said. Perhaps I was lucky for him.'

Jock II growled in his sleep. He didn't like his dreams being disturbed. There were more cats invading the gardens, big ones, small ones, black, tabby, tortoiseshell, grey, brown, long-haired, short-haired . . . cats from so many countries, from all over the world, from an English garden party, from his constituency in Dundee, from Sidney Street, from nights of the blitz, from the banks of the Nile . . .

Suddenly Jock II could stand it no longer. He leaped to his feet and with a great bound he sent the cats scattering in all directions. Some ran into bushes, some shot up trees, some vanished straight into the lake. He chased them out of the garden, back into the mists from which they had come.

'Good heavens,' said a visitor watching from the bow-window of the study. 'Whatever's gotten into that cat?'

One of the lady guides came to the door with his supper dish. 'Jock, Jock,' she called. 'It's supper time.'

Jock II stopped in his wild tracks; the garden was empty now. He sniffed the clean Kent air. Then he slicked down his tawny fur and regained his composure before returning to the house for his supper-time audience. Chartwell was back to normal.

The Highland Hunter

Towser lived in the still house. It is normally very warm, but in deference to her great age, she also has her own electric fire on twenty-four hours a day.

She emerges from her bed located under a big onion-shaped copper still and stretches herself, shaking out her magnificent tortoiseshell fur. She is a long-haired cat with orange and black fur, tabby markings on a sweet, gentle face, and a white bib. Her long white whiskers twitch in anticipation of breakfast.

She is totally unaware of her champion status and that her photograph is on the cover of the *Guinness Book of Records* for 1984 in full colour – and that it also appears on the back cover of this book!

Her life is spent prowling the dark wooden halls of Glenturret and the forested hills that surround the ancient distillery. Breathing in the whisky-laden fumes is as natural to Towser as inhaling the crisp Highland mountain air that blows down the slopes.

The huddle of two-hundred-year-old whitewashed stone buildings has been her home since kittenhood. She was born behind a wash charger, a big warm container that was the perfect hiding place for the four kittens. The stillman had been hunting for Colette, the mother cat, when he found the kittens.

As soon as she was big enough, Towser began exploring the rambling distillery, up and down stairs and steps, along the many passageways. Once she found a room full of grain that was nice and warm, but then she could not find her way back to her mother. She was completely lost. The same stillman found her.

'Are you lost, wee kitten?' he said, scooping her up in his big hand.

Transforming the barley into a smooth Scotch malt is a long slow process; it ages for fifteen years in the huge oak casks. The rich smells from the distillery promise a feast of top-quality barley for families of woodmice descending in droves from the heathery hills.

It was not long before the kitten caught a mouse bigger than herself. This mouse changed the direction of Towser's life.

'We need a really good mouser to help Colette,' said the stillman. 'We ought to keep you.'

So Towser followed in the pawprints of her ancestors, who had patrolled Glenturret since 1775 when the distilling of whisky began on the banks of the tumbling River Turret, near the Scottish market town of Crieff.

She would not dream of missing her daily dram of whisky. It was every drop as good as a saucer of milk. She loved the taste, curling her tongue round the last sip of vein-tingling golden liquid. It was always a fifteen-year-old malt, but no one thought it wasted on a cat. Towser earned her dram.

Towser thought it was a day like any other day. She sniffed the fumes of the 130-degree-proof malt and it went straight to her head. She prowled her domain in the sheds storing barley, purring and growling softly through her sharp teeth. There would be breakfast waiting for her in the canteen, but first she had work to do.

It was all too easy, almost like swatting flies. She sat as still as a statue until her long white whiskers signalled a sighting. She pounced. Victory! A mouse dangled lifelessly from her jaws. She went on a triumphal parade with her trophy, growling at anyone who might dare to take her catch away.

Charlie got out a sheet of paper and a pencil.

'One,' he said, marking it on that day's log.

For a number of weeks they had been keeping track of Towser's mousing. It began as a joke, but as the tally rose, the distillery workers realised that they had a potential champion under their roof. Towser was catching an average of three a day; but she also caught pheasants and baby rabbits when she escaped from the distillery and raced to the dark roots and wet mosses of the woods, her shaggy coat flying in the bitter Perthshire wind.

There was a workforce of six at this time so there was always someone who had an eye on Towser's activities. She pounced. Again!

'Another mouse. Aye, chalk it up, lad.'

Towser crouched in the shadows of the pipes carrying water, steam and whisky. She knew there was a nest somewhere near but it was well hidden. She decided to try a little subterfuge. She climbed up onto the pipes to take a nonchalant walk. It was a tricky balancing act, not made easy by the alcoholic fumes fuzzing her keen eyesight. But she was a sure-footed alcoholic, practically weaned on whisky.

She dived off the pipe, fast as an arrow, silent as a ghost; her paws cupped the mouse delicately in a death thrust.

'Another one. How many's that now?'

'Three. And all before breakfast.'

It was not long before word went round the distillery that Towser was onto a winning streak. The tally rose steadily . . . four, five, six.

'This is amazing,' said Peter Fairlie, the managing director as he made his morning round of the distillery. 'We've got a real champion here. It must be the fumes that keep her fit for the job!'

For Towser was now no young cat in her prime. She was already twenty years old and had been catching the Glenturret mice all her life.

She became aware that she was being watched. Visitors were nothing unusual for more than 70,000 people a year toured the distillery, enjoying the occasional glimpse of her orange and black fur. Towser was happy to be the centre of attraction, stroked by her admirers. Sometimes she sat in the picnic area, watching the arrival of the cars and coaches, unashamedly cadging treats from the picnickers.

This was different. She was being shadowed. The stalker was being stalked and it was an uncanny feeling. She peered over her shoulder. A pair of jeans were not far behind. She blinked in case it was the whisky. But no, she was being followed by a pair of jeans.

She was intrigued, mystified. She took them on a fair old dance, behind casks, under pipes and through gullies, clambering over mountainous sacks of barley, through fanlights, over roofs, and into every dark corner. Her yellow eyes brightened with a gleam of mischief. It was something to do with hunting, she felt sure.

She pounced on an idle dormouse. Wham! She hid her catch neatly under a pile of sacks. That was one they weren't going to know about.

The day's happy hunting continued. The blue jeans, obviously exhausted, were replaced by a pair of white sneakers. She took them on another wild-mouse chase. It was such fun. She was almost giddy with excitement. She was chasing around the distillery, fur rumpled, her long plume of a tail carried high like a flowing banner.

'That cat's tiddly,' said Mr Fairlie, as if it was the most normal thing in the world.

Towser came back, a little wobbly on her feet, growling a low throaty sound, another victim in her jaws. She laid it at his feet as a gift.

'Thank you, Towser,' he said.

'Fourteen,' shouted Hugh triumphantly. 'Fourteen mice in one day! It's a record.'

Towser grinned smugly. Little did they know.

She took the next day off. All morning she lay draped dangerously over a pipe, letting the frail sun warm her fur. Later she ran across the fields that rose from the cluster of buildings, through the trees and up rolling heather-clad hills into the Highland mountains, a bird's eye view above the still loch and swiftly running River Earn.

Her ancestors had lived wild in the hills, she knew that. The knowledge pounded through her veins. She ran like the great cat she was, shaggy coat flying, big paws hardly touching the ground, every muscle moving in perfect coordination.

Down below in the distillery, the workforce had their calculators out. They reckoned that Towser caught an average of three mice a day. It did not sound much as a bare fact. But some bright spark was multiplying that by her age and came up with the astounding total kill to date of over 22,500 mice.

'Twenty-two thousand mice? You must be daft.'

'Work it out for yourself. She's twenty years old. Multiply the number of days she's lived by three, and that's the answer. I reckon she's the world's top mouser.'

The world's top mouser yawned and blinked against the mountain wind and thought about a nice saucer of her favourite condensed milk. She did not know that they were contacting the editors of the *Guinness Book of Records*; that a new cottage industry was about to spring up, with tee-shirts and mugs, life-size posters and post-cards of the champion, newspaper interviews, TV appearances and a fan club.

She wandered down to the distillery. She wanted her wee dram, and the warmth of her electric fire on her back. She was beginning to feel her age.

Towser was billed as the greatest mouser on record in the *Guinness Book of Records*, and the 1984 *Guinness Book of Pet Records* acknowledged a total kill of 23,000 mice. Journalists came to get the inside story. Often she kept them waiting; then brought them a mouse as a peace offering.

In April 1985, Towser indirectly received a letter from the Queen. They had something in common. They shared the same birthday, 21 April.

The Queen's Private Secretary wrote from Windsor Castle saying that the Queen hoped that Towser, like herself, would celebrate the day with all possible happiness.

Photographers came to take birthday pictures of the grand old lady – Towser, not the Queen. Towser loved every minute of it. She was used to this admiration. And for a twenty-two-year-old (154 cat years), she was keeping her good looks. Her coat was still beautiful and fluffy, her prowess at hunting unimpaired.

But something was amiss. Earlier that day she had fallen off a steam pipe which she had walked safely every day of her life. She had almost fallen into a wash-back container. Hanging on by her claws, she managed to pull herself up. It was not the alcoholic fumes, for she was nowhere near the stills, and she had not had her daily dram. She was not in the least pie-eyed.

Towser righted herself and shook out her fur, pretending that she had intended to jump anyway. No one had noticed. She was aware of something wrong with one eye. Puzzled and blinking, she began washing carefully with a curved paw, hoping to wash away the irritating blur. Eventually she gave up. Nothing seemed to make any difference. Perhaps she would sleep, and when she woke up the mist would have gone.

Birthday cards arrived from as far away as America, Canada, Australia and New Zealand. That evening there was going to be a party in her honour. She wouldn't miss a party. She would keep awake for that.

It was a grand party, but Towser got a little carried away with high spirits. She jumped out onto a window ledge and along a gutter, then climbed the sloping roof to the top of the distillery. It was an exciting, mad birthday gesture. She was twenty-two years old! She wanted to admire the sky and glory in the magnificent Highland panorama.

It was very exhilarating, the wind streaming through her long fur, until Towser decided it was time to come down. It seemed far steeper going down than it had coming up. Somehow the roof had changed. Towser found she could not get down. Apprehensively she looked around for another route and sniffed the air. She could smell thunder in the distance, and already grey clouds were gathering overhead. There was going to be a storm.

She panicked and began yowling, loudly and insistently. People came out into the yard, talking and pointing upwards to where Towser was perched on the roof, silhouetted against the sky.

She heard the scrape of a ladder and a familiar voice saying: 'Okay, Towser. It's all right. I'll get you down in a minute.'

It was her old friend, the stillman. He clambered over the roof, put Towser inside his warm tweed jacket and took her safely back to earth.

Some days later she was patrolling her territory when suddenly she saw a mouse. She was after it like lightning, across the still house, out into the yard. A van from the *Strathearn Herald* swerved wildly and slammed on emergency brakes. The driver got out, shaking, while Towser continued in hot pursuit of her prey.

'I nearly ran over your ch-champion c-cat,' stammered Peter MacSporran, the driver. 'Why doesn't she look where's she going?'

'Because she's almost blind in her left eye,' said Peter Fairlie coming out of his office. 'When she runs from right to left she can't see what's coming. But she doesn't seem to know it, and keeps on mouse hunting with as much vigour as ever.'

'And I nearly ran her over!' Peter MacSporran had had a terrible fright.

'Come and have a wee dram to settle your nerves,' said Mr Fairlie.

Towser pounced on the cheeky mouse and held it down with one big furry paw. That was mouse number twenty-five thousand, two hundred and seventy-seven. They weren't the only ones who could count.

Top Cat

There was such a lot of fuss about this thing called Christmas. Streamers he mustn't play with; presents he mustn't sit on; decorations he mustn't chew . . . Sammy was fed up with Christmas before it had even begun. He was used to being the focus of attention and now Christmas – whatever that was – was uppermost in everyone's thoughts. Was it another cat? If so, Sammy wasn't having it. There was only room for one cat in his household.

Sammy sat watching the driving rain from the comfort of a windowsill. The weather was appalling, even for December. He decided not to go out until it was a sheer necessity. If he was bored he would go and play with Danny's toys or stalk that spider that lurked on the landing. He might just have a little snooze.

It was dark when he awoke. Time for a stretch, a quick wash-and-brush-up of his long, elegant ginger and white fur, a flick of his long whiskers and he was ready for supper.

'I haven't had time to cook your coley,' said Christine. 'You'll have to make do with a tin. I've been so busy Christmas shopping.'

After his supper, Sammy wandered outside. The family were all preoccupied with what they were going to buy for Christmas, make for Christmas, do for Christmas. This Christmas person must be very important, Sammy thought.

His thoughts were still bobbing around when he noticed that he had wandered further afield than normal. The houses were all strange ones and the streets smelt different. He circled warily, trying to pick up a familiar scent.

Suddenly a pair of yellow eyes confronted him; then bared, snarling long teeth. Sammy leapt back, adrenalin pumping. Another deep growl from behind froze him in his tracks. Sammy hissed, fluffing out his fur to make himself look twice his size, tail thrashing.

But Sammy wasn't fooling anyone. He was still only cat-size, and the dogs were big, dirty and hungry. They knew they had him cornered and they crouched, ready to attack, sharp claws rasping on the slippery paving stones.

Sammy made an instant decision. He fled. He cleared the nearest dog with one bound and ran for his life. He did not know which direction to take. The terrifying chase took him further and further from home. It was alien country. The dogs yelped at his heels, getting closer as their longer strides narrowed the gap.

Sammy found himself in a big yard. He was panting and tiring rapidly. He knew he couldn't go on much longer; he must find some refuge, preferably a very tall tree. Something huge was ahead of him. He had never seen anything so tall and dark and menacing. It soared into the sky like a tree, but it was a giant, branchless tree, its tip lost in the rain-laden clouds. But there was not a leaf in sight.

There was no time to wonder what it was; the dogs were almost upon him. Sammy took a flying leap onto the lowest rung of a ladder which was bolted to the side of the tall structure. His claws slipped on the wet rungs, but with supercat strength born of sheer terror, he hauled himself up out of reach of the snapping jaws.

It was a narrow, slippery perch, even for a cat. He

climbed a little higher, hoping for something rather more substantial. There seemed to be more than one ladder, each twice as long as a man, overlapping, and where they overlapped the double width of rung gave Sammy more of a pawhold. He settled on a double rung for the night, the rain pelting him from all angles, stinging his eyes. He tucked his nose miserably into his wet fur and wished he were at home. He felt the first pangs of hunger in his stomach.

The dogs were milling around below, sniffing, snarling, confident that their prey would have to come down. They barked noisily in the mill yard, intoxicated by all the new smells, eventually finding places to shelter from the cold and rain.

Sammy crouched, motionless, thinking about this massive, inhospitable, silent tree. No leaves, no frisky birds, no nice rustling sound; just an impassive giant planted in the ground by some super being from the sky.

He sniffed. He smelt soot and brickwork. Bricks meant a wall. It was a tall round wall. How strange. It was certainly not a house. He had never seen a house that had no windows or doors and reached up into the clouds. But at least the bricks accounted for the lack of branches and leaves. Soothed by that little bit of reasoning, Sammy closed his eyes again and tried to sleep.

It was a bitterly cold December night; when dawn eventually crept unwillingly into the frosty sky, Sammy's wet fur was stiff with ice-white crystals. His limbs ached with coldness. He stretched himself unsteadily, longing for a good leap and run across gardens, hedges and railings.

He saw the dark shapes below of the dogs lolling in sleep, yawning and scratching. There was nowhere to go but up.

Perhaps there might be somewhere, up there. His heart lightened and this encouraging thought spurred his climb. The round wall looked as if it went straight into the sky, but it might not. He passed a derelict bird's nest pathetically stuffed into a crevice. Nothing in it but a few old spiders. He didn't eat spiders; not yet anyway.

Some schoolchildren saw him first. They shouted and waved.

'Puss, puss, puss.'

'Poor thing.'

'C'mon, superman.'

Sammy took no notice. He was not feeling sociable. He climbed a few rungs higher.

The mill yard was coming to life. Workers began to arrive by car, on motorbikes, bicycles, on foot. By now Sammy was a ginger blob half way up the chimney. He was very frightened by all the noise and commotion below. He was hungry. He licked some of the moisture off his fur, longing for a saucer of warm milk.

He peered down. It was a very long way. People were blurs of muddy colours, all heads. He couldn't see the dogs; perhaps he would take a chance and go down. He turned stiffly, each paw placed with care on the cold, rusty rung. It was breakfast time and he had missed a late-night supper.

It was then that Sammy discovered he couldn't go down. It was nothing like a tree, he couldn't leap from branch to branch in a zig-zag route downwards. He squinted at the rung below, trying to puzzle out how to reach it. The blood rushed to his head and his vision blurred. It was impossible. The rung was flat, almost non-existent. He was stuck.

Fear raced through him. What could he do? He leaped a few rungs higher in his panic, vaguely aware of a wave of sound from the ground.

'Look! That's a cat! Half way up the chimney.'

'Cripes. It's stuck all right.'

'Call the fire brigade.'

'How about the RSPCA? They'd know what to do.'

'What about the steeplejack. You know . . .?'

'Fred.'

'That's him. The one that's on the telly. Fred Dibnah.'

Fred Dibnah was a television celebrity, made famous by his steepleclimbing programmes. Sammy knew nothing about all that; he knew nothing about the news cameras arriving, being flashed skywards and popping off photos of him; he knew nothing of the television lens being focused on the chimney and the commentator interviewing anyone who would say anything.

'It gave me a real fright,' said a girl, bright magenta hair gelled out to porcupine spikes. 'I looked up the chimney and I said to my friend: "Look, Grace, there's a cat up the chimney." That's what I said. I don't know how it got there.'

'Have you any idea how it got up there?' asked the reporter, keeping to his basic line of questions. He whipped the microphone back to her glossy lips.

'No,' she said, shaking her head carefully. 'It climbed up there, I suppose.'

Luckily Fred Dibnah was already at the mill, preparing to start some scheduled chimney-repair work. He collected his tackle and strode through the crowd at the foot of the chimney. He could just make out a gingery blob about a hundred feet up the steel ladders, two thirds of its height.

'I hope it doesn't bite,' he said jovially, strapping on his harness.

By now Sammy was terrified out of his wits. He was not going to let anyone within scratching distance. Instinct made him take the only action left to him . . . to climb higher and higher, rung by rung. The wind combed fiercely through his fur; the ladder creaked and seemed to sway.

Suddenly there was no more ladder to climb. Sammy was amazed. He was at the top. It was another strange place. Cautiously he crawled onto a narrow ledge, stretching his stiff legs in their first real movement for hours. He inched himself slowly round the ledge, blinking against the gale that howled like banshees around the top of the chimney.

77

He was hardly able to appreciate the view of Greater Manchester stretching into the dim grey Lancashire distance. An endless vista of factories, power stations, housing estates, church spires and cooling towers became a blur. He peered tremulously over the inner edge . . . down, down into a black void that plummeted into the very core of the earth. Sammy shivered. It smelt acrid and stale. He knew its darkness was dangerous.

'Don't be frightened. There, there, there, puss, puss, puss,' called Fred encouragingly, peering up from the ladder below the top. 'Come along now, good pussy. Come to Fred.'

Sammy wasn't coming to Fred. He wasn't going to anyone. He was too terrified to move, crouched aloft, watching the man with fixed, staring eyes as if he was an alien creature from outer space.

'I've a nice bit of sardine for you,' Fred tempted. 'How about some sardines from the canteen? Come along, old boy. Come on, ginger.'

Sammy's stomach was gnawing with hunger, but his taste-buds acted on smell, not words. He could not tell what Fred was waving about. Fred had brought up a wire mesh basket, tied to his waist. Sammy did not like the look of it . . . baskets meant captivity and visits to the vet.

Fred proffered more tempting morsels from the canteen, wishing the cat would make up its mind. Conditions were very unpleasant, with driving rain and a fierce wind. Even with his skill and experience of high buildings, this was no picnic.

Sammy flattened his ears to cut down wind resistance and huddled into his fur. The day wore on; television crews came and went. Fred threw sardines around, most missing the ledge and dropping onto spectators' heads.

A cameraman removed a sardine from the peak of his cap. 'I know it rains cats and dogs in Manchester,' he said. 'But fish is ridiculous.'

As the light began to fade, Fred came down, shaking

his head. It was too dangerous now to stay aloft, or even try another attempt that afternoon. Sammy was doomed to another night . . . if he didn't fall off.

While millions of television viewers watched the drama of the rescue attempts on the news in the comfort and central heating of their homes, Sammy was slowly freezing into a hump of abject misery. Only his long fur saved him, and the pockets of warm air still trapped in its wetness. He pushed his nose into what little warmth he could find and tried to concentrate on not being blown off his perch by the bitter wind.

He had found a tangle of rope securing some tackle to the brickwork, and dug his claws into the fibres. It was the only thing he could cling to. His frozen spirit put him onto automatic pilot as he hung on through the long night.

When dawn of the second day came, the weather had not abated. The driving rain still stung, the wind still howled and buffeted the top. Even Fred queried the wisdom of attempting another climb in such conditions, but the plight of Lofty – as Sammy had been christened by the media – had caught the imagination of the country. He was front-page news in most of the national newspapers.

Fred did not like the thought of the cat slowly starving to death 150 feet above Bolton. He would have one more try. He fastened on his cumbersome harness and started the climb.

'Come along, Lofty, now,' he coaxed, holding out a morsel of cold chicken saved by the canteen staff for their most reluctant customer. 'Nice puss. You don't want to stay up here in this nasty old place, do you? Don't you want to go home?'

Sammy did want to go home, but by now he was frozen, both with fright and cold. A second night aloft had reduced him to a shaking bundle of confusion. He defied Fred's entreaties without knowing why. He refused food despite his raging hunger and thirst. He clung relentlessly to the rope, only once forsaking it – to retreat further round the ledge when Fred got too close.

Fred jammed his cap firmly over his tingling ears and began the descent. It was time to knock off for a bite to eat and a pint of beer at the pub. His hands were frozen and it would need nimble fingers to catch that cat.

'I can't make him budge,' he said sadly.

A crowd of mill workers gathered below the chimney in their lunch-hour. It was drama on their doorstep. They craned their necks to catch sight of the tiny silhouette of pointed ears just visible against the sky.

The weather was deteriorating even further. The whiplash rain soaked spectators in minutes. But they hung around, stamping their feet, waiting for something to happen. Gerry Rodgers stood silent among the crowd. It was his lunch-break from a nearby rubber factory. He liked cats. He hoped to see the ginger cat rescued.

He tipped his head back. The chimney was the tallest, blackest, most frightening thing he had ever seen. The ladders crawled up the outside, disappearing into infinity. It towered above him like a monster from some disaster movie.

Suddenly Gerry made up his mind. Steeling his nerves, he raced to the chimney and shot up the first ladder. He climbed quickly, allowing no time to think, no time to look down, keeping his eyes fixed only on the rung above. He climbed, hand over hand, with relentless determination.

Gasps went up from the crowd. Time and again his green wellies slipped on the wet rungs, but he clung on, using the strength in his wrists till he gained a surer foothold. Rain plastered his dark fringe to his forehead. His clothes were soaked. The howling wind filled his ears with unholy ferocity. All this, he thought wryly, for a scrap of ginger fur.

He caught his breath at the top, and heaved himself onto the ledge, panting. He was thirty years old, but at that moment he felt about ninety. He could see the cat, its fur flattened and sodden. It looked as terrified as Gerry felt.

'Puss, puss, puss,' he called gently, the wind whipping his words away to the distant grey hills. 'I won't hurt you.'

But Sammy was not moving for Gerry either.

'Come along . . . you can trust me. I'll get you down.'

For thirty minutes Gerry sweet-talked the cat to come near enough to grab him. But he was always just that bit out of reach. Gerry clung to the top ledge, so cold he could hardly think. He could not stay there much longer.

A sudden gust nudged Sammy along a few inches. It was a chance movement that brought him within reach of Gerry's long arms.

Sammy felt himself grabbed by the scruff of his neck. He was swung off his safe perch. He found himself struggling in mid-air, all four paws windmilling like fury. The rain lashed at his eyes and a blurred panorama of sky, brickwork and bearded man whirled before him. He went wild with terror. He was being carried down with an awkward, jerking movement. The man descended painstakingly, rung at a time, using only one hand to hang onto the side of the ladder, the weather-bitten steel rasping his skin.

The other hand held the cat in a vice-like grip. Sammy fought the hand and arm that held him, unable to realise what was happening. It was all part of the nightmare. His bedraggled tail waved in a furious question mark.

'Now, now, pussy. Don't struggle or you'll have us both off.'

They were forty feet from the ground when Fred came back from his beer break. He hurried to hoist the wire animal basket up to Gerry on a rope. Gerry bundled the cat, head first and upside-down into the basket and slammed the lid. He leaned back onto the ladder with relief. His wrist was numbed and aching with pain; he could not have held on much longer.

Sammy huddled into the swaying cage as it was

lowered gently towards the ground. He dug his claws into the wire mesh as he swung in the air. He felt horribly exposed. He saw crowds of people below; they were getting bigger . . . policemen, camera crews, reporters, factory workers. What were they all staring at?

A terrific cheer went up as the cage bumped onto the ground, then the crowd broke into spontaneous applause. Gerry felt his knees buckle as his green wellies stepped off the last rung and touched the firm yard beneath. He straightened himself, grinning, aware that he was shaking.

The police were waiting for Gerry – but not with congratulations. It was an offence to climb someone else's chimney, even to rescue a cat.

'We shan't charge you,' said the police officer. 'But you're an idiot. No insurance, no harness.'

'I saw the cat on the television last night,' said Gerry, as if that was reason enough.

'Were you scared?' asked a reporter.

Gerry looked back up at the 150-foot chimney and its dwindling rim in the mist.

'I tried not to look down,' he said with a shudder.

Sammy was taken to the RSPCA van parked nearby. Someone was rubbing him gently with a towel. They were pouring milk into a saucer. There was the delicious smell of food being unwrapped. Chicken, fish, liver . . . Sammy didn't care what it was.

As his tongue curled round the milk, he nearly choked in his eagerness. He lapped and lapped, knowing the delicious smells were all for him when he had slaked his thirst. He began to purr. He couldn't help it, because now he had his answer. Now he knew what Christmas was.

Hamlet on West Forty-fourth Street

I am a New York City street kid on the up and up. And I don't just mean riding the old-fashioned elevators of the Algonquin Hotel on New York's Forty-fourth Street and Fifth Avenue, but in the company I was now keeping. Writers, directors, producers, actors and actresses of stage and screen, journalists and gossip writers . . . they were glamour and class and everyone a celebrity.

Their haunt is my haunt . . . no, my home. I am a personage of some distinction, but careful not to let my origins slip. Nothing escapes my notice in this haven of genial companionship.

I guess it's a dollar to a dime that I was born in a carrier bag downtown. The seamier streets were my scratching ground and I latched onto a gang of wild ferals that terrorised any paunchy dog that dared to set a reckless paw on our territory. Then some cat groupies reckoned I was fitted for a better life and hauled me off to the Bide-a-Wee Society for Stray Animals' rescue home. That was me rescued. Was I grateful? Not likely.

In a swift counter attack they de-loused, de-fleaed and shampooed me inside out. I was so clean, I squeaked. It was a big leap from streets to sanitisation, which I bore with much fortitude.

Then some inspired lady novelist between books comes along and transports me in her automobile. I clawed my way out of the box and leaped onto the passenger seat. I'd diced with death in half of New York's traffic and I was not going to be intimidated by a red Volkswagen.

'Calm down, buster,' she said as she drove towards Manhattan. 'You're going to a very nice place and I want you all in one piece. You're for the high life if you behave. This hotel is the tops in New York. It's the pulse of New York's literary circle.'

I didn't let on I had no idea what she was talking about. My old neighbourhood was grey with sleazy rooming houses that called themselves hotels. They paid giants to throw things at cats.

'Someone has seen a mouse in the vicinity of the Algonquin and it's a red-alert situation,' she went on.

I decided to stake out this hotel. It is in the heart of mid-town Manhattan. I was jaunty as a sailor on a forty-eighter as we went in through the front portals, below the fluttering Stars and Stripes. What a shock was in store. It took my breath away.

I knew immediately I was in some special, superior joint. The air of grandeur, the elegance, the antique porcelain lamps glowing from the dark pillars, the grand furniture and smell of good polish. I tiptoed over the thick carpet as the grandfather clock discreetly ticked away the silent minutes . . . it was an island of old-world calm that I never knew even existed. A very long way from the antiseptic Bide-a-Wee.

My racoon-striped tail began to tingle with excitement. A single-minded determination seeded and grew. I would own what I saw. I would brook no rivals, no mangy street cat was coming within a mile of my hotel. I would become an equal to the great. I would be a celebrity in my own right.

'This is your new cat,' said the lady novelist.

The exact nature of the hotel was at first mystifying.

Under the floor, the boiler throbbed night and day. People came and went, preceded or followed by bellboys carrying luggage of different shapes and sizes, sometimes escorted by the bell captain in his brown and gold striped uniform. I saw no purpose whatsoever in this daily parade.

Another puzzlement was the crowd of people who came regularly for cocktails at six in the Blue Bar. It filled with literary agents and editors in a migratory wave as their offices closed. They did not bring luggage, only manuscripts. But the ritual of going through the crowded oak-panelled lobby was a must, whatever.

Cocktail hour was the tops. I crunched my way through snacklets dropped or sneaked to me by a surreptitious hand. I was always ready for the odd shrimp or slice of smoked salmon. And I could retreat and observe the human traffic from my favourite spot half way between the elevator and the grandfather clock, tucked away under a low sofa.

I gained the reputation of being a big sleeper, but was I asleep? No. I was merely listening with my eyes half closed, an air of royal aloofness disguising my curiosity. The scandal was amazing. Sometimes I had to remove myself from it all and curl up on the special shelf over Harry's news-stand on a stack of copies of the *Soho News*. One can only take so much.

I had my own door to the kitchen, but some guy had put the wrong name over the flap. A little sign said 'Rusty' and it creaked of long ago cat. Sometimes I had this dream of Rusty, a tortoiseshell tom, and we had tricky and near the knuckle conversations about the hotel guests. I learned a lot from Rusty. We had this understanding.

Talking of kitchens, the food was five-star. Chicken and cream, prawns and puddings. Gourmet. When I think of the trashcan pickings I was brought up on! But I was still street wise. I drank straight from the tap, even in the best company.

There were three dining rooms in the hotel, the Rose Room, the Chinese Room and the Oak Room. I wasn't fussy. Once I took my own mouse into the ruby-panelled dining room but no one was grateful. The women shrieked and hitched up their skirts, painted faces reflecting their horror in the mirrored walls. The chandeliers tinkled in the hot-air thermal of gasps. The head waiter told me off with a wagging finger.

'No mice allowed in the dining room, Hamlet,' he said sternly, removing the offending corpse. I growled. I was outraged. I was only trying to help. I thought he was my friend. They were so busy in the dining room with a post-theatre buffet. Did they want me to eat on the hotel steps like a vagrant?

From that day, I was barred from the dining room.

'Tut, tut, Hamlet,' said the reception clerk kindly as my eye swivelled in the direction of soft lights and starched tablecloths. 'You know you're not allowed in.'

I flicked my tail haughtily. It was no skin off my nose. Not with a name like Hamlet. Shakespearean, I was told, but it still sounded half way to a pork and egg fry. Some name for a handsome white and grey lynx cat, with a large white head and sharp amber eyes that can kill at five yards.

So they thought I was a big sleeper; I was a big nipper and that was no mean rumour, buddy. I was really hung-up on a dainty curved female ankle that I could clamp onto with both paws. How I loved to creep up under a sofa and suddenly fasten my claws onto an unsuspecting ankle. I reckon the stocking trade ought to pay me an honorarium.

Male ankles were not so much fun. Females forgave me as I pretended I was sorry and purred into their hands. Men just swore. I soon discovered that there was a vulnerable two inches of pale hairless skin above short socks that was extremely vulnerable. I could spot an unguarded shin at a hundred yards; crawl towards it under sofas, coffee tables and chairs, silent as a spider as they discussed and argued about the theatrical and literary world outside. Suddenly I would pounce on my prey. His sharp yelp could be heard well above the chatter. Heads swivelled in the electric silence, craning at the culprit. It was very satisfying.

Being famous didn't mean no certificate of exemption. An ankle was an ankle. I bit 'em in the order in which they walked through my royal domain; it was the price they paid.

Don't think I didn't pay my price. No more street brawls. No more nights on the town. No more stalking dark alleyways with my pals.

But the Algonquin was mine. Any time. All the time. I rode in elevators, snoozed in linen carts, and if I was sure no one was looking, jogged along the maze of corridors on the upper floors.

Otherwise my demeanour was dignified, a shade haughty, stopping to greet guests, to pass the time of day, to reassure a nervous newcomer, welcome an old friend, my tail pointing up and curling in an elegant manner befitting my surroundings.

I was ambassador to the rich and not so rich, to the famous and to those who had not made it yet. Sir Laurence Olivier, Burt Reynolds, Albert Finney, Erica Jong, Peter Ustinov, Jeremy Irons, Anthony Andrews . . . they were all good for a tickle under the chin, a scratch on the head.

The past was another ball game. They say that the *New Yorker* magazine was born within these walls. Dorothy Parker, Robert Benchley, George S. Kaufman, Alexander Woollcott . . . I could sense these literary ghosts still sitting on the plump velvet chairs. They formed what was called a Round Table of wits that met at the hotel, but I never saw any such table. And I kept my eyes skinned.

Critics say I'm a snooty cat but that's just sour Bourbon, and a lack of understanding of the feline character. I keep my distance, like any self-respecting cat. I've seen enough dogs that fawn and ingratiate at their master's feet like there was no tomorrow. I get interviewed for television. They write about me in newspapers from coast to coast. I'm filmed with the cast at the Algonquin for a movie. Guests send me postcards and souvenirs from all over the world, photographs and gifts. Some joker sent me a little bell for my collar. They don't do all that for no snooty cat.

The cocktail-set told me that Rusty used to sip his milk from a champagne glass in the Blue Bar. So what? That's no big deal. I got my own style. I'm no cheap imitation. Besides, I got perception. I can tell when a new fresh-faced actress from the woods has got that special oomph . . . I can spot a writer with excitement leaking out of his eyes, casting around the lobby for the right face to talk to.

'I got it just right today, Hamlet,' he'd say, bending down to tell me. 'Wish me luck.'

'Who's here today, Hamlet,' she'd whisper, stroking my ears. 'Who's casting around? What did they say?'

A couple of times a week I'd saunter into the managing director's book-lined office, enjoying the literary ambiance. If only I could share my thoughts with him. Mr Anspach looks up from his executive desk, a contemplative twinkle in his eyes. People are always writing to him about me.

'I wish you'd answer your own letters,' he grins, tweaking my tail.

I've been lord cat of the hotel lobby a long time now. It must be nearly ten, twelve, fourteen years. I can't count and I don't bite so good anymore. Time is mellowing my fierce nature. The old clock and I tick on, measuring the minutes, watching the flow of humans through half-closed eyes.

Who would guess that I nearly didn't stay on after that first Christmas at the hotel? I almost snuck back to the streets of New York City on a night that I will never forget.

True, they had some kind of party going on. There had

been parties going on and off ever since Thanksgiving Day. My friends from stage and screen were wining and dining, talking, laughing, having fun. I'd eaten so much I had roast turkey coming out of my ears. I could barely squeeze my huge bulk under my favourite sofa to sleep it off.

I was slipping down the hazy corridors of sleep, chasing pigeons over the rooftops of Manhattan with Rusty in my winter dream, when suddenly, as the grandfather clock chimed midnight, an ear-shattering pandemonium broke out in the hotel.

My fur stood on end.

The swing doors from the kitchens were flung back. A chain of shrieking white devils came writhing in a snake-dance through the lobby, clanging and banging pots and pans in wild abandon. The sound was cataplectic; it shook the windows, split the air waves, woke the long-dead fossils entombed in the hotel's foundations.

I froze with terror, cowering back under the sofa, the din attacking my delicate eardrums until I could have screeched with the agony.

The devil spirits danced past me, white-faced masks grinning, their banging and clanging vibrating along every jagged nerve-end of my body. If I could have moved, I would have fled. All the way to Coney Island.

They told me afterwards, when they finally managed to drag me out from under the sofa, that it was only the waiters and bellboys dressed up with tablecloths over their heads. But I knew better. I was street wise. Hadn't I come up from the pits? I seen a devil or two before . . .

'Sorry, Hamlet old chap,' said Andrew Anspach, trying to reassure me. 'We forgot to warn you. It's an old Algonquin tradition on New Year's Eve. We have to make sure no evil spirits are lurking around the hotel that might cause mischief in the coming year.'

'It's a tradition you could well discontinue,' said a lady guest, nursing her bruised ears.

'We're afraid to take the chance,' said Mr Anspach with an amiable shrug.

It took several saucers of cream to calm my shattered nerves. Okay, I could deal with hotel mice, dogs, chase away wavering shadows that might scare a late guest creeping along to his room, but those New Year devils are something else. Each year I got to take cover, curl my tail over my nose, shut my eyes tight and make out I'm not there.

When the ear-splitting uproar and tour of the hotel rooms is over, and the festivities settle back into near normalcy, I come out of my hiding place, first making sure it's all clear. Not a devil in sight.

I shake out my fur and my tail, have a quick lick and brush-up, and then after several deep breaths, join our partying guests as if nothing untoward has happened.

And that's a cat acting, buddy. Straight off Broadway.

Scraps

(Adapted from an account by Mrs Olivia M. Slobbé)

He was the tiniest kitten of the litter and the last one left, an ebony black scrap of humanity, clawing at the empty air. No one wanted him. He was going to be drowned.

They had never thought of owning a cat. They were staying with her brother prior to moving to New Malden to their first house. The kitten looked so weak and appealing that they took him home. Anton, who was Dutch, had been in hospital for two years after the war and had only just started a job in the City.

'We can't really afford to have a cat,' said Anton.

'But we could feed him on scraps from the table,' said Olivia, wanting the kitten. 'He's so tiny and helpless.' Cat first, furniture later . . . her priorities were in that order.

They took Scraps to New Malden in the back of the van, on Olivia's lap. They did not have a cat basket. The kitten slept all the way.

It was a glorious August day, hot and still. They put Scraps on the lawn while they moved their belongings out of the van. The garden was an enchanted place. All they could see of Scraps was the tip of his black tail as he tentatively explored the jungle of weeds and grass.

Olivia and Anton set up home with the bare necessities. They had two beds, a piano (a legacy from Anton's mother), a statue of Nell Gwynn, an alarm clock and a set of fish knives and forks. Now they also had a cat.

Scraps was supposed to be fed from scraps from the table. He did not know but he sometimes ate better than they did. It was 1948 and rationing was still in force. Nor did he think it strange that they ate from the closed lid of the piano while they were saving for a table.

He was so tiny he could hardly climb the stairs and had to be lifted round the bend onto the landing. They took turns during the night to fill the hot-water bottle for his bed. He grew into a fastidious cat; he would not use his litter box if it was dirty; he would only eat off a clean plate.

Eventually Olivia got a job and Scraps was always waiting by the door for her return. She would get on her hands and knees for a few moments of rapturous reunion.

'Has it been a long, long day?' said Olivia, putting her face into the soft, glossy fur, knowing he would never put out his claws. 'When you've been neutered you'll be able to explore the wide world. We'll teach you how to come and go through the fanlight. Then you'll be free to do as you please.'

They began to teach him with a piece of string how to get onto the shed and jump through the fanlight. It was a wonderful game and Scraps thought it great fun. He was taught to jump down onto a low cupboard inside and then onto the floor. It took some time for Scraps to master this involved route, but they were patient and he was bright and intelligent.

He was light on his feet. He sprang through the fanlight with the nimbleness of an Olympic gymnastic gold-medallist. It was a joy to watch the performance.

Till the day Olivia forgot to open the fanlight.

Scraps knocked himself out. He lay unconscious on the

floor, the world black and reeling, kitten-size stars before his eyes.

Olivia was horrified. How did one revive an unconscious cat? She cuddled him on her knees until he was less dazed, then gave him some milk.

He didn't forget. He regarded the fanlight with apprehension and it was some time before he could be encouraged to use it again. It was back to square one with the piece of string until he gained confidence. But he always made sure it was open first.

How they enjoyed that first summer in their home. They quickly became a close family, the three of them, playing hide and seek in the garden like children during the long light evenings.

'Where's Scraps?' they would call. 'Where's Scraps?'

A tiny black streak would tear out of the bushes, touch ankles with his nose, then bound off to hide again. The garden was one immense playground for Scraps. Anton built a trellis to hide the bottom of the garden, but they all secretly thought that the part they were hiding was the loveliest. It was a wild paradise of tangled blackberry bushes, fragrant apple trees, blackcurrant bushes and raspberry canes.

Whenever they took a walk down the local lane, Scraps came too. He did not want to be left behind. He was never far from them, yet never ventured anywhere on his own. Malden was already becoming a suburban estate, although the village itself was quaint and pretty.

Scraps developed a sweet tooth, but only for home-made cakes. He scorned shop cake. He sat on Anton's knee to share his tea; when he thought no one was looking he would swiftly hook his paw round a piece of cake from Anton's plate. Delicious. He liked queen cakes, and sponges, but shortbread was his favourite.

While he was still small he sat on Anton's shoulder for the morning ritual of shaving. Perhaps he thought the lather was a sponge mix. He liked to lick the lather from Anton's face.

'Leave off,' grinned Anton into the mirror. A small black, foam-smudged face peered back.

Scraps invented a marvellous game along the hall passage, a sort of cat ski-run. It was a Saturday and Sunday game, when Anton and Olivia were both at home and all three doors would be open.

He would take off from the front gate, gallop along the path gathering momentum, leap onto the runner and slide along the polished floor all the way into the kitchen and out of the back door. He could also do this in reverse, from the back door to the front garden. It was exhilarating. But also exhausting. After three or four runs Scraps would flop down, flaked out, panting like a dog.

Winter turned the passage into an icy blast and Scraps liked warmth. He stopped asking for the doors to be opened. There was no central heating in those days, and the game stopped.

They did not go out much as they were saving up to buy furniture. They couldn't go on eating off the piano lid forever. But one evening they decided to go to the cinema.

'The one-and-nines?' Anton suggested.

'How lovely,' said Olivia, fetching her coat.

Scraps sat alone in the empty house. They had gone out without him. How could they? He always went on their walks. How could he convey his utter disgust that they had deserted him?

He was too gentle a creature to actually cause any damage. It was not in his nature. But somehow he had to communicate the depth of his feelings. He wandered around the rooms wondering what he could do. It is not easy for a cat to get a message over to human owners.

Olivia loved flowers. They grew mostly vegetables but because it was spring and daffodils were cheap, she had treated herself to a dozen golden-headed blooms. They stood, glorious and glowing, in a vase on the piano.

Scraps jumped onto the piano and very carefully, with his head on one side, put his mouth gently round a stem

94

and lifted it out of the vase. He moved delicately because he did not want to knock over the vase or spill water on Olivia's piano top.

He laid the extracted daffodil on the piano and went back for a second. It took him a long time to remove all twelve flowers. He laid them in a row along the top and retreated to the top of the stairs, feeling pleased with himself. He had made a statement. That would teach them for going out without him.

They came back late, laughing and talking about the film. Scraps sat at the top of the stairs, dignified and remote, not coming down to greet them as he usually would. Olivia was too happy after the unexpected outing to take much notice. She went to put the kettle on for a cup of coffee.

When she went into the dining room and saw the row of daffodils laid along the top of the piano, she knew why Scraps was looking smug.

'The young monkey,' she laughed. 'Anton, come and look at this. See what Scrap's been up to. He obviously didn't approve of our going out. Hey, Scraps, are you coming off your high horse for some warm milk?'

It was some weeks before they had the temerity to go out again. They had forgotten the daffodil incident, but Scraps hadn't. When he discovered that they had gone out without him again, he couldn't believe it. He roamed around the house, his thoughts in a turmoil. Perhaps they hadn't understood . . .

A recent purchase had been a second-hand table for the hall which Olivia had polished and polished until it shone. On it she had put a bowl of dried flowers. Scraps decided to make the same protest, but with a little variation.

When Olivia and Anton returned from visiting her parents they found a dried flower placed on each step of the stairs and Scraps sitting at the top awaiting their return, the same smug expression on his face.

'Okay, Scraps, we get the message,' said Anton, much

amused. 'How about putting them back in the bowl if you are such a clever cat, eh?'

They did not try leaving Scraps again. They even took him electioneering, delivering pamphlets door to door in the village. One woman asked them in. Scraps took a strong objection to the delay and sat on her doorstep howling like a coyote. They had to make a hurried retreat.

'That's no way to win votes,' said Olivia, shooing him down the path. His glossy black tail shot up in greeting. He had only wanted to see them. Even a few minutes' separation was too much.

Some Saturdays Anton went to watch Chelsea playing. Scraps always seemed to know on which train he was returning, for the cat would move from the fire onto the windowsill to watch for his arrival. It was Olivia's cue to put the kettle on, and Scraps was always right. Moments later Anton would walk in.

'Our Lord and Master returning home from his gallivanting,' said Olivia to the cat with a secret smile as they both went to meet him.

They grew into a devoted family, a threesome. Scraps hated being away from them for any length of time. They insisted that he slept in his own sleeping box in the kitchen, but relented enough to take him to bed for a last game of pictures on the wall.

They made shadow pictures of rabbits and dogs on the wall with their fingers. Scraps watched, fascinated, occasionally unable to resist a leap and a paw at the moving pictures.

'No more,' said Anton yawning. 'It's bedtime. Even yours, young Scraps.'

'The show's over,' said Olivia firmly, taking Scraps downstairs. 'No more television. You're a lucky puss; you have a television but we don't!'

Nor did they need an alarm clock, for Scraps woke them each morning with a gentle paw on each eyelid. He waited on a small ledge in their bedroom, watching the early morning birds flying past, wishing he could catch one but knowing instinctively that he would be reprimanded. He did not get told off for taking a nap in the airing cupboard, tucked away among the towels. He knew what he could do and could not do.

He could tell them when he was hungry and wanted to eat. They had taught him how to open the larder door by hooking his paw round the edge and pulling it open. Scraps would go in, take off the cloth that covered his plate of fish or liver and carry the cloth to Olivia, waving it like the trophy of some fierce jungle hunter.

'Thank you, Scraps,' said Olivia, taking the cloth from his jaws. 'Would you like your breakfast?'

He never took the food. After all, he wanted a clean plate. He was fussy.

One day when Anton and Olivia returned home from work, Scraps was not there to greet them. It was so unusual, they looked at each other with unspoken fears. He did not come home that night or the night after.

They searched the house and the garden and the nearby lane, becoming more and more frantic with worry. He had never stayed out before.

'I can't think of anything that would make Scraps stay away from us for even one night,' said Olivia, over and over again. She could not concentrate on anything. She kept thinking of their little black cat, so small and sweet, and how he must be feeling. 'Something must have happened to him.'

It was autumn and the weather was crisp and dry. They searched as far as they could go, asking everyone they met if they had seen a small, glossy black cat . . . A young couple, desperate to find the tiny scrap who had become so much part of their lives.

'He's wearing his medallion so perhaps someone will bring him back,' said Olivia, clutching at straws.

'He wouldn't have gone with anyone. He must have been stolen,' said Anton, chilled by the thought of people's cruelty. That lovely glossy black fur had a price.

Scraps had been very wary of anyone strange since the day burglars broke into their house. They had stolen Olivia's engagement ring and Anton's suit.

Scraps had seen it all, hiding beneath Anton's wardrobe. At first even Olivia could not persuade him to come out; for a long while he never left their side, following them like a black shadow. They shut the fanlight for a time and Scraps knew why. He had seen how the burglars got in . . . He had seen the boy wriggling through and knew something was very wrong.

'He would never have gone off with a stranger,' they agreed.

'I miss him so much . . .'

'Wc both do,' said Anton, comforting his young wife.

The next evening they were sitting in their dining room. By now they had saved enough to buy a dining-room suite and two fireside chairs, but that night they took no pleasure in their new furniture. They were worrying about Scraps and wondering what had happened to him.

Suddenly they heard a familiar sound. The tiny scratch, the light landing of paws, the creak of wood. It was Scraps coming in through the fanlight.

'It's Scraps,' whispered Olivia, hardly daring to hope. He did not come through to them. They waited.

'Scraps?' Anton called. But he did not come.

They went out into the kitchen. Scraps was sitting on the back door mat, plastered from head to foot in thick brown mud. It had dried on him and his tail was as stiff as a board and sticking up like a beanpole. He looked utterly dejected and weary.

'Oh my poor, poor darling,' said Olivia, going down on her knees to hug the bedraggled cat, mud and all. She felt a quiver run along his tired body. Somehow he had got himself home.

He allowed himself to be shampooed in the kitchen sink, something which he had never let Olivia do before.

He knew he had to get clean, and he could not do it himself. Wrapped in a warm towel and cuddled in front of the fire, he began a low purr, which grew and grew as if he would never stop. He was home. He was really home with them again.

Scraps had obviously fallen into some stagnant pond. But there was no pond for miles around and the ditches were all dry. If only Scraps could tell them where he had been taken, but they would never know. When his fur was dry, Anton brushed him gently with an old army hairbrush, and put him to bed. He slept the sleep of the exhausted, but they took it in turns to creep down the stairs to look at him.

When winter came, they sat each evening by the coal fire. Scraps invented a new game. He would sit with his head in a paper bag. How he purred, loving the warmth. It was nice inside the paper bag and it shut out the electric light. He had got the idea at Christmas when Olivia and Anton were opening their presents and the floor was strewn with paper.

One of his Christmas presents was a piece of ribbon which Olivia would tie onto his tail. Rolling over and over, he could untie the ribbon and take it to them, asking to start the game all over again. The paper bag and the ribbon at the same time was a special party trick.

'If only we could take a photo of him,' laughed Olivia.

Olivia was the pianist of the family. Scraps knew what he liked. He liked 'When Irish Eyes are Smiling' and 'Peg of my Heart'. But if Olivia began to play the popular song 'Mares Eat Oats and Does Eat Oats and Little Lambs Eat Ivy', he would jump up onto the piano and march along the piano keys in a highly successful wrecking operation.

It had been two years of working hard and saving to get their home together, and the following year Olivia and Anton planned to take a holiday, their first.

They booked two weeks at a holiday camp at Bracklesham Bay, and left Scraps at a cats' home, kissing his sweet nose goodbye when they left.

'Now be very good Scraps and we'll soon be back,' said Olivia.

It was a wonderful holiday, all thoughts of the desert war, the pain, the years in hospital, began to fade into the past. They walked along the steeply shelving pebble beach, watching the waves pounding the shore, listening to the music of the sea. When they returned home, they immediately went to fetch Scraps. He came before anything.

The little cat went wild with excitement when he saw Olivia and Anton. Purring, climbing over them, nudging chins, kneading, burrowing deep into their arms, all with little cries of joy. But they were shocked by the change in their cat's appearance. He was desperately thin.

'He pined and wouldn't eat,' said the owner of the cats' home, shaking her head. 'We couldn't get him to eat at all.'

The happiness of their holiday fled, melting like butter in that summer's sun. They wished they had never gone. The taste of the spray was bitter now. They took Scraps home, tenderly nursing the sick cat all that night and the following day. But Scraps had been the tiniest and weakest of the litter. His heart, valiant and courageous enough to find his weary way home after being stolen, could no longer take the strain.

He was cradled in Anton's arms when he breathed a last sigh and was gone.

He died of a broken heart, believing that they had left him. The vet said this too.

Olivia cried and cried. Scraps had been like a child. She couldn't believe he had gone, that sweet, glossy black little cat. It was heart-breaking.

For weeks they could not bear to go back to an empty house. They walked about every evening and did not eat. Nor could they have him buried in the garden where they had spent so many happy hours playing with their little black friend.

The local police buried Scraps in the garden at the back of the police station where he would be safe forever. They never had another cat. Scraps could not be replaced.

Rescue in Venice

It was late evening when the plane from England landed at Milan airport, and 1 a.m. before they arrived outside Venice. Thick fog swirled round the Piazzale Roma at the end of the causeway, turning the magical city into a strange, unwelcoming and eerie place.

Damp rose from the canals in the chill January air. Mrs Helena Sanders shivered despite her warm clothes. The Cornwall she had just left had been warmer. For a moment she wished she was back in her cosy house overlooking the estuary; then she stiffened her resolve. They were here on a rescue mission.

She and Miss Mabel Raymonde-Hawkins and her photographer were weighed down with luggage; two cat traps, a pile of collapsible pussy-packs and photographic equipment. They were well prepared for this second visit to Venice.

They huddled together, the fog blanketing them from the real world. Footsteps on the wet flagstones came and went but they saw no one. It was only too easy to imagine ghosts of long-departed Doges flitting through the narrow passageways . . .

'Let's find a hotel for what's left of the night,' said Mrs Sanders briskly.

'What a good idea,' said Miss Raymonde-Hawkins with relief.

Next morning they caught a water bus travelling the entire length of the Grand Canal to the small hotel where they had booked rooms.

The long chugging ride down the winding Grand Canal was a dazzling dream-like experience even in mid-January. The pink and gilded marble palaces glided by, two hundred monumental palazzos of the wealthy merchants and Doges, the sea lapping the crumbling green-mildewed landing steps and blackened piles. The wash from the boat splashed relentlessly against the ancient stone buildings. How beautiful it looked in the cold luminosity of the pale grey morning light.

Mrs Sanders sat back to enjoy these last tranquil moments before the fight began. She knew it was going to be a fight. She had no illusions about anything being easy.

It was nearly two years since her first visit to Venice, in the summer of 1964, and that long-awaited holiday with her husband had been ruined by the misery they saw.

Swarms of emaciated and dying cats lay everywhere. Starving and diseased, they infested the city. If Mrs Sanders saw ten dying cats on one side, she saw twelve on the other. And this was Venice, Queen of the Adriatic, city of sixteenth-century magnificence, city of glorious disrepair, slowly sinking, drowning in its own beauty . . .

She had thrown a piece of ham to a cat so starved that its ribs were sticking out. But it was too weak to eat.

The sights sickened her. It was a dying city, its buildings dying, its cats dying. She had to do something. But she lived in Cornwall. How could someone living in Cornwall rescue the estimated 68,000 feral cats living in Venice?

The first cats were brought to Venice by a Doge to keep down the rats that crept in from the canals. They were ownerless, municipal rat-catchers, deliberately introduced to control plague. They lived all over the place, in gardens, under bridges, in the squares, the markets, in cellars. They bred rapidly in the maze of peeling-paint alley-ways, beneath the festoons of washing hung from iron balconies.

The authorities turned a blind eye despite the usefulness of the rat-catching cats. They ignored the dying, the diseased, the maimed, the pitiful starving kittens. The cats were prisoners in Venice. They could not escape to the countryside. There are only two dry ways out of Venice; one by a very busy motorway, the other by train from St Lucia station – neither recognisable cat tracks.

As the water bus neared the landing stage at St Mark's Square, Mrs Sanders caught sight of a headline in the *Gazzetino*: 'THE WHOLE TOWN IS LAUGHING AT THE CAT SAFARI'.

She had been afraid they might get a bad press. One of the English tabloids had got hold of the wrong idea and printed a story saying that they were going to hire a gondola, put a big cage in it and pay old women a hundred lire to give them cats. It was ludicrous.

Later there had been a cartoon in the *Corriere della Sera* and a leader headlined: 'DANGEROUS TIMES FOR THE CATS OF VENICE'.

The impression given by the paper was that they wanted to kill all the cats because they hated them.

Mrs Sanders knew it was going to be uphill work to organise their mercy mission. They wanted to make a drastic attempt to reduce the cat population by euthanasia, neutering and spaying by authorised vets, as well as supporting the existing system of cat women to feed the cats.

'Helena,' said Miss Raymonde-Hawkins. 'Who are all those people on the landing stage? Is it some kind of riot?'

Mrs Sanders saw a crowd of people milling around. She hoped they were not who she thought they were. At the approach of the water bus, the crowd began to jostle for positions in the firing line.

'It's a posse,' said Mrs Sanders. 'A posse of journalists.'

The Italian press were lying in wait; so were journalists from many other countries.

The director of the Italian Animal Welfare Organisation, known as ENPA, was furious. He said he had mobilised all eighteen of his inspectors, cancelling all leave and keeping them on emergency duty. Later he admitted that this was not true.

'If Mrs Sanders ill-treats one cat she will have to face the full majesty of Italian law,' he announced to the media.

The journalists pressed in on the two women they thought were coming to massacre the cats. It was a frightening moment, but Mrs Sanders and Miss Raymonde-Hawkins were not deterred. They were not totally alone. They had friends in Venice. There were people who cared and had been trying to get help for some time.

The two women could hardly walk because of the press. Photographers lay on the ground to get shots; reporters harassed them with microphones held to their lips to catch every word.

'Can't you get rid of all these people?' Mrs Sanders anxiously asked two policemen.

The officer shrugged his shoulders. 'You are celebrities,' he said.

During their visit one of the Venetian supporters accused the director of the ENPA of not supporting the English cat women. The director complained to the police. The two women were summoned to appear before the head of the Aliens Department. For half an hour he shouted at them. It was very unnerving.

'Why do you come to this country to break the law?' he bellowed.

'In which country is it illegal to take a sick animal to the vet?' Mrs Sanders shouted back. She tried shouting some more but it had little effect. It was a difficult situation.

Eventually he calmed down, Mrs Sanders explaining

in Italian the real purpose of their visit to Venice. He called in the director of ENPA, who kissed their hands and showed them to the door. They were free.

As soon as they were safely at a distance from the police station, they collapsed in helpless giggles and had to lean against a wall. The next day they flew home.

It was not the end of their work; it was the beginning. They left behind an organisation of cat women: selected, trustworthy old women who gave their time and money to feeding the cats. They were given veterinary forms which said in Italian: 'Please sterilise/give veterinary treatment/put down.'

They made arrangements with an Italian vet who agreed to spay, neuter, treat or destroy for his usual fee. Gradually the cat women started to take cats to the vet.

There was no first cat that was treated; there were only swarms. Among the first was a dying cat, his eyes and nose congealed with discharge from 'flu. He could neither see nor smell and was unaware that a plate of food was beside him.

The cats in the Rialto fish market were so hungry they were eating the paper in which the fish had been wrapped. January was a bad time for cats. Most of the hotels were closed and that source of food was denied them.

The main priority now was to raise money. It came from many different people and organisations; just enough to keep paying the bills.

Mrs Sanders returned to Cornwall to find she had made the headlines in the *Western Morning News*: 'TRURO WOMAN ARRESTED BY VENICE POLICE' and 'VENETIAN POLICE FOLLOW TRURO CAT WOMAN' then later 'APPALLING CAT CRUELTY IN VENICE ALLEGED'.

Miss Raymonde-Hawkins, who was already busy enough running the Raystede Animal Centre in Sussex and was planning to work for the Irish tinkers' equines, hoped to hand over to the Venetians, but it soon became obvious they had no plans to continue the work. It was an expensive scheme because of the enormous numbers of cats.

A new horror emerged during their third visit, in October 1966. The authorities planned to spend £70,000 on poisoning the rats with phosphorus, a poison which burns up an animal. A cat eating such a poisoned rat would die an agonising death. Mrs Sanders and her friends rushed to Venice to appeal to the Mayor of Venice and to the newspapers to publicise this horrendous plan. But the press had lost interest in cats.

The day before they left for home, the plan was abandoned and the lorries, already in Venice loaded with phosphorus, were sent back to Milan.

The following day the disastrous 1966 flood deluged the area. It swept through Venice, drowning many cats. But rats also drowned and so the cats' food supply was further diminished.

Mrs Sanders immediately rang the Italian Red Cross to ask what they needed. She collected two tons of bedding and warm clothing for the people of Venice, and a thousand tins of KiteKat. She organised ten tons of free freight space and gave surplus shipping space to the Anglo–Italian Society for the Protection of Animals to accommodate supplies of calf food to the flooded Po valley. The Italian customs held up the consignment because of the donated cat food; a sympathetic Venetian paid the considerable duty on this.

It was obvious that the rescue group had to be properly organised. Mrs Sanders sent out eight hundred letters to lawyers, clergy, doctors and accountants in Venice; eight people replied positively.

On 1 November 1969, the documents inaugurating DINGO as a registered charity were signed. Dingo was the name of a little stray dog rescued by Gina Fieri, the painter, better known as Gina Scarpabolla. It was a word which could be pronounced easily by speakers of both languages.

For several years DINGO treated about four hundred

cats a year. Then in 1982 the work doubled. It was estimated that when their rescue work began there were 68,000 ferals in Venice; their number now is between 4000 and 5000.

Many of the cats are astonishingly tame. They like spaghetti. They stroll among the tourists. They sit beside the busy canals, not afraid of being kicked in. They traverse the burnt-red roof-tops with familiarity, knowing the nooks for sunbathing and the crannies to shelter from the rain.

The cat women still feed the cats, take the sick and injured to the vet's, collect new-born kittens to be put down and where possible take cats to be spayed. Their dedication is not easy. They are liable to abuse, ridicule and sometimes even violence.

In 1985 the Venetian DINGO was formed. It was a thrilling moment for Mrs Sanders, twenty years after her first mission, to be in a Venetian lawyer's office, putting her signature to an Italian document transferring responsibility to Venetian DINGO.

It was a very hot day in May. There was a dinner in the open air, the gift of a gold chain and two long legal documents about the principles behind DINGO. She thought of the thousands of cats they had rescued and treated, and the current colonies now healthier and cared for. And all against such odds. They had come a long way from that foggy night in January 1966. She remembered the cold fog swirling round them and the hostile press. It had not been easy.

On 26 May 1985, a colourful ceremony was held in the medieval heart of Venice. In the Church of San Moisè behind St Mark's Square, near the pink and white marble of the Doge's Palace, Mrs Helena Sanders of Truro, Cornwall, England, was made a member of the Order of the Knights of St Mark. It was a most distinguished honour.

She arrived again, with Miss Raymonde-Hawkins and

Peter Bluck, her photographer, at Marco Polo airport. This time they were met by animal-lovers with a car and bouquets of flowers.

Several Knights, wearing their white cloaks and the bifurcated blue enamel cross of St Mark's, were gathered in the ornate Renaissance church. Mrs Sanders was the first to be led before the Doge by her sponsor. She was taken in front of the congregation and the citation was read.

The Doge put the St Mark's Cross round her neck, saying: 'I admit you to the Knights of St Mark in the name of our Holy Patron. Be a good citizen.'

Then a lady Knight pinned on a buttonhole with a miniature badge and put the white cloak round Mrs Sanders' shoulders. She is one of the very few British people to be so honoured.

Afterwards there was Mass and a sermon, then a party with wine and cocktail snacks. It was very hot and Mrs Sanders was in some discomfort. Her feet had swelled and her almost new shoes were killing her.

Later she hobbled back to the hotel and kicked them off.

'No more tight shoes for me,' she said firmly.

After that she went round Venice in old bedroom slippers with a hole in them, anxious to see how her big family fared.

A colony of cats races up and down steps and over the city's hump-backed bridges, their black and tabby coats gleaming with health, eyes round with curiosity. They sit by the canals, watching the river traffic; the slow gondolas, the chugging vaporetti, the sleek water taxis, bows polished and gleaming, speeding noisily for the lagoon.

They regard the tourists with well-bred indifference, the swarms of pigeons in St Mark's Square with calculated tolerance.

They are Mrs Sanders' real reward.

Cat in Court

Mijbil sat at the window of the small flat in Ryde, watching – entranced by the outside world. She was fascinated by everything that she could not reach . . . grass, raindrops, scuttling leaves, the scurrying clouds, birds sweeping the vast sky with such enviable freedom.

She was too well mannered to sigh but she longed for a garden to play in. It was difficult to play in the flat without colliding with something, either the two children or the new Abyssinian kitten, Simba.

Her mistress understood. The flat imprisoned her too. She often took the cats out into the countryside or to the woods on the Isle of Wight so that they could have a romp. It was so exciting, going in the car, then being let loose to sniff and stalk, to leap and bound about in abandon. They never ran away.

Mijbil had come to the family as a temporary guest, a small, skinny, flea-ridden little black scrap. All eyes and ears and sharp little pin-pointed claws, almost too small to survive. She was going to be a surprise for a neighbour's child.

But the little black scrap knew where she belonged. She followed the family everywhere, purring and vibrating with love, till everyone fell utterly and devastatingly in love with her.

She grew strong and brave and it was this bravado that earned her such a strange name. She was fascinated by water and loved to dabble her paws, breaking up the shimmering reflections.

The family were in a swimming pool, splashing about, and she wanted to join them; she ran round the edge, nearer and nearer, then suddenly she was in the pool, paddling her splayed-out paws frantically towards her mistress.

'Silly puss,' said the woman, swimming towards her and pulling the kitten out of the water. 'What do you think you are – an otter?'

So she was called Mijbil, after the otter in *Ring of Bright Water*.

Mij and Simba were used to being taken out on harnesses and leads, but Mij loved travelling in the car most of all. The back window was her favourite place for watching the traffic flashing past, the trees waving branches overhead, wobbly cyclists and thundering lorries. She would sit there, safe and secure, purring, not minding the bumps as the ancient Morris 1000 took them towards the countryside.

'Come along, Mij. We're going visiting friends. It's a lovely sunny day. We ought to be outside enjoying it.'

Mij needed no second telling. She leaped down from the windowsill and twisted her sleek black body round her mistress's ankles. She was sure the friends would have a garden and she could spend a long, glorious afternoon chasing bees and flies and those fluttering butterflies.

They sang as they chugged over the downs in the warm, dappled April sunshine. The children and their mother sang pop songs while Mij purred an accompaniment that lulled Simba to sleep.

The Morris joined the main road and approached a big roundabout. There was an orange car coming from the right, so they slowed and stopped.

Mij was curious. She was always curious about everything. She climbed over onto her mistress's lap and looked out of the window to see if it was someone she knew. She arched her sleek black back, her golden eyes bright with speculation.

She was a little disappointed that it was a stranger in the other car. A man in a dark blue uniform with a woman and child. He drove round the roundabout and went down a road in the opposite direction.

Their car started again and they drove towards their friend's home, unaware that fate was about to take a hand in the proceedings.

Oddly enough, the orange car reappeared. It was right behind them. Mij spotted it first, then her mistress saw the car in the mirror. The woman drove especially carefully now, aware that the old car was conspicuous by the very fact of its age. She kept to a steady 35 m.p.h. The orange car stayed behind them.

'Oh dear,' she said, beginning to feel apprehensive. 'What a nuisance. There's a policeman in the car behind me and I want to turn right and these old-fashioned indicators don't work.'

Everyone swivelled round and stared at the orange car that was still following them.

'I'll go really slowly, then maybe he'll pass me.'

But he didn't. He stayed a steady, regulation twenty-five feet away.

'Mummy, he's tailing us!' the children shrieked. 'How exciting.'

'It is not exciting. It's worrying.'

Mij was aware of the rising tension in the car but could not understand it. What was a policeman? The cat was more interested in a small insect that was trapped in a corner of the car, buzzing around helplessly.

There was a slight jolt as the car stopped. What was happening? Her mistress got out. The orange car pulled round in front of them and the policeman got out too. Mij tore her attention away from the bug to inspect the new arrival. She was always interested in new people . . . perhaps he had come to make friends.

There were further, harder jolts as the policeman kicked all the wheels of the Morris. No, he definitely hadn't come to make friends.

'I'll have to caution you for driving without due care and attention,' he said, scowling at the rusting body-work.

'I beg your pardon?'

'Don't you know it's an offence to travel with animals loose in the car?' he went on.

Mij listened with faint surprise. She thought about all the dogs she'd seen leaping about in the backs of cars, not to mention children quarrelling and fighting and crying. Mij felt quite indignant. She was not a loose animal. And Simba was still fast asleep, a fat bundle of apricot-coloured fluff.

Mij, the kitten and the children enjoyed their visit to the friend's house, but the woman seemed deflated and dejected. She was obviously worried about the incident.

'Don't worry,' said their solicitor later. 'The sergeant will throw it out of the window and tell the constable not to be ridiculous.'

But he didn't. A summons arrived and their mistress was ordered to appear in court. A mantle of gloom fell on the family's happiness. The woman was worried. At the last moment she picked up Mij and put the cat in her travelling basket.

'Mij is involved so she'd better come along too,' she told their friend Pat, who was going to keep them company in court. 'The whole thing seems so ridiculous and such a waste of court time and money. They might as well see my lovely Mij, see the kind of cat they are complaining about.'

Mij did not mind. It was another outing. Another chance to see something new. This court place might be interesting with things to chase and new delicious things to sniff. It would be heaps better than staying in the flat.

113

Cat and owner sat outside Newport court, their thought-waves of apprehension and panic almost bouncing off the walls. Mij's mistress was wondering if she had done the right thing in bringing the cat to court. Would it be thought in contempt? Mij had no such doubts. She was with her beloved mistress and that could only be right.

'You are a good, well-behaved little thing, aren't you?' Mij was asked.

'For a moment I thought you meant me,' said a friendly policeman sitting in front of them. He was dark-haired and good-looking. 'What are you up for?'

'I'm not really sure.'

'I'll find out for you,' he offered. He went up to the prosecuting officer and returned with a huge grin on his tanned face. 'You're up for Driving in an Illegal Position!'

Mij felt her mistress relax a little as she and her friend Pat laughed. She was very curious about the place to which she had been taken. There was not a pot plant in sight, let alone a garden.

The case began. The courtroom was packed. The dark wood of the raised bench where the magistrate sat seemed threatening. In front of it sat the clerk of the court, rustling through his papers.

Mij began to enjoy herself despite the nervousness of the two women. There were such nice people around her, saying sweet things to her in her basket. She peered around with interest, noting the high bleak windows, wondering when she would be allowed out to explore.

Police Officer Roger Blench was giving evidence in the box. Mij recognised him as the one who had kicked the wheels of the car.

'First of all I want to say that I could not fault the defendant's driving,' he began. 'I drew onto the roundabout on the main East Cowes road and I saw the cat with its forepaws resting on the front window ledge.'

'Excuse me,' interrupted Mr Francis Eade, the magistrate. 'Do you mean forepaws or four paws?'

Mij heard the laughter sweep through the room. Yes, this really was a very jolly place with everyone laughing.

'Oh, only its forepaws, sir – the cat was on the lady's lap as she drove her car. He seemed to be looking out of the window,' said PC Blench. 'I then noticed two children and a second cat in the car as well.'

Pat testified as to Mij's perfect behaviour in the car, then her mistress had a turn to speak.

'Mij is an experienced car traveller and she enjoys it,' she told the court. 'I have learned a lesson, and so have many other people I've asked who did not know it was an offence to have a cat on your lap while driving.'

The magistrate listened gravely, his thin, lined face expressionless. 'As I understand we have the culprit in court, perhaps we had better have a look at her,' he said.

Mij looked around alertly, ears perked, as she was carried to the Bench and put down in front of the magistrate. Perhaps this was when she would be allowed to start exploring? Mr Eade came face to face with Mij's golden eyes and their amber-flecked depths held him in a long gaze. Mij certainly knew how to behave. She rubbed her head against the wire front of the basket in a friendly way.

Mr Eade hesitantly put his finger through the wire and tickled Mij under her small pointed chin. She purred with appreciation and nudged him gently, asking for her ears to be rubbed as well. His face softened, a smile threatened to break the normal gravity of his expression.

'Ah . . . er, well . . . yes,' he said at last. 'She's . . . er, obviously a very well-behaved cat . . . but as the case has been brought to court, and if the situation had arisen where, er . . .' His voice grew gruffer. 'Then Mij could have got in the way, causing an accident. It is, therefore, I'm afraid, necessary to fine you the minimum, nominal fine of £5. But do please keep her in a basket in future.'

'Yes. Thank you. I will.'

115

Mij added her thanks, quite reluctant to leave her new friend, to whom she had taken a shine. But the press were waiting and she realised by now that she was of prime interest to everyone – quite a celebrity, in fact. There was still a lot to be said for leaping and chasing ants and bumble bees and flies in the long grass, but Mij reckoned that her appearance in court was a totally unique experience for a cat.

That evening Southern TV ran the story. Mij was somewhat less impressed by this part of the proceedings. She did not even recognise herself on the box.

Outside there was a cloud that looked just like a bird hovering, ready to swoop on a prey. Mij ran along the windowsill, her eyes gleaming, whiskers twitching like radar, her long black tail held high. It might just be a bird and she might just catch it.

The Siamese Traveller

He came as a gift from another tea planter's wife, a creamy scrap of wild spitting and clawing that fitted into her hand. There was a dog in the household and since Chinky had never seen himself, he decided early in life that he was of the same species.

'Chinky,' they said, exasperated by his dog-like nips and bites. 'If you are going to behave like a dog, then you are going to be trained like a dog. And there's no need to glare at us! The first word you're going to learn is NO.'

Chinky had no trouble learning; he just had to copy the dog. Sit, beg, come . . . it was easy. Chinky prowled restlessly. He wanted something to sink his fangs into, something to do that was bold and fierce.

In the tea country in Assam, acre upon acre of plantations and rolling hills are cut with neat rows of green tea bushes edged with virgin jungle. The low evergreen shrubs shaded by tall leguminous flowering trees were an ideal playground for Chinky. It was fun but tame. He was a full-grown cat now and sat among the lush grass, tail flicking, watching the men who were coming to tidy the memsahib's garden. They were simple and poor but with the natural grace of their people; the sweeping movement of their *kadhalis* caught his eye.

In the distance is the country of the Nagas, the short

117

stocky hill people who lived in the thickly covered and almost impenetrable ranges of great hills, beyond which is Burma and then the ancient land of Siam. It is one of the wettest places in the world during the monsoon, hot and humid in the day. But it has a cold–weather season when the days are misty and evocative of England.

Chinky watched the workers walking slowly up the hill; his eyes narrowed. Suddenly Chinky leaped out, back arched, legs stiff, claws unsheathed, an unearthly Siamese yowl coming from clenched jaws. His ears flattened back, and with his tail raised high, he began an elaborate sideways dance, moving in a circle round the terrified men. Their eyes widened with fright. They had never seen such a small, fierce creature. Perhaps it was a demon!

All work ceased. They dropped tools on the ground in horror. Chinky danced round them, the sun sparkling on his short creamy fur, his blue eyes flashing like brilliant gems. His teeth bared. It was an awesome sight.

'Yee . . . ow,' he screeched.

They backed away. They knew about tigers, but when they saw Chinky's unsheathed claws, they could not be sure that it was not a new and dangerous species.

'Now, now, Chinky,' laughed the memsahib, lifting him up into the air, not afraid of his windmill paws. 'That was very naughty and I'm ashamed of you.'

Chinky grinned smugly. He was not in the least ashamed. He would do it again if he got the chance. And he did, every morning, until the men were less afraid and grew used to his wild tribal dance. Then it was no fun any more.

He had an amazing uncatlike speed. Arrow fast, he could beat memsahib to the veranda even after hiding in the flower beds and giving her a head start to the veranda steps.

The Assamese girls, wicker baskets strapped to their heads, worked their way from bush to bush skilfully plucking just the tip and two leaves from across the dark compact bushes. They were used to Chinky's antics.

'Bulbac Billi,' they giggled to each other and covered their mouths with their colourful saris. They thought he was like a clown, so they called him a clown cat.

Chinky did not think he was funny; he thought he was fierce. This warrior spirit made him heedless of danger. Each snake hole was examined with an investigative paw. He caught one of the silly, wriggly things and brought it back to the bungalow, its shiny black body curling on each side of his mouth like a mandarin's moustache. The memsahib was definitely not amused.

'No thank you, Chinky,' she said firmly, wanting the snake removed quickly. 'No snakes today or any day. And certainly not indoors please.'

Chinky took his prize outside in a huff. Humans were peculiar. He relaxed his jaws and the snake slithered away into the undergrowth. Chinky growled deeply in his throat. He had to find bigger and more exciting prey. His nerves tingled with the excitement of a fight.

He had to go where the action was. He embarked on the first of his travels . . . not far by human scale but a long way for a small Siamese. He strolled through the hut village where the workers lived and the tea factory compound, past the Indian clerks' brick houses and the great leaf-withering sheds.

A big wooden barn loomed ahead. It was the rice godown. Chinky smelt danger. A thousand tiny eyes pierced the darkness. Chinky stiffened and then pounced. Got it!

For four days they searched for him, scouring the large garden and the tea estate, walking along between the rows of tea bushes, calling his name and peering underneath. They began to dread that he had been taken by a leopard.

The factory engineer found Chinky in the godown, surrounded by his kill of rats and mice. He was wild with hunting. They couldn't catch him. He evaded them like quicksilver, a streak of pale fur in the gloomy darkness.

Eventually they tricked him into a box and nailed the lid down.

Chinky spat and yowled continuously all the way home in the lorry. He was furious. How dare they? This was no way for a triumphant warrior to return, in a box. He demanded to be let out.

He was eventually let out at the bungalow, but despite the great fuss made of him, he was still spitting and scratching. Nailed down in a box . . . the indignity, the humiliation. He would have nothing to do with anyone.

'How on earth are we going to get Chinky back to England?' said the memsahib. 'None of our friends will have Chinky even as a gift. He's far too much of a handful.'

'If he thinks he's a dog, let's treat him like a dog,' said the sahib, producing a lead.

Chinky eyed the lead suspiciously. He already wore a collar, but what was this? They started walking him round the garden on the lead. They called it lessons. Again it was pretty tame. They took him on practice car rides as a passenger, but not caged in a box or basket. He refused point blank to travel in a basket.

He liked to roam in the car, exhibiting his superior power of balance as they bumped over the rough tracks, always watching as they drove along the edge of the true jungle. He really liked being a traveller.

They had bought him a basket with a hinged lid. He sniffed at it, smelling the human hands that had woven the cane. They were local prisoners from Jorhat . . . prisoners making a prison for another. Chinky treated it with caution.

There was a great deal of activity going on, packing cases and crates strewn with crunchy paper and wood-shavings. Chinky tried to help with the packing, exploring the boxes, getting in the way.

'Chinky, will you please get out of that box? You are not travelling with my best china.'

Tail high, Chinky retreated into the garden. Whatever

was going on, he wanted nothing more to do with it.

He did not know they were leaving India, his home for years. The word meant nothing to him. But he was interested in the drive from the Hunwal tea estate to Jorhat airfield. He stood with his paws on the dashboard, eyes agog at the new sights along the road – the water buffalo, the cyclists, vans and lorries jostling along the roadway, bright saris fluttering in the wind, the scent of the Brahmaputra river.

At Jorhat airfield, Chinky was almost speechless with amazement. But not quite. The great silver Dakota did not frighten him. It was only another kind of bird . . . another way to travel.

It was even more exciting than hearing a tiger dragging a water buffalo after the kill. When the plane took off, he viewed the dwindling land below with star-bright eyes, paws kneading the arm of the cabin seat in a kind of tribal rhythm. This was really living.

His behaviour during the flight was impeccable. The memsahib was relieved. She had imagined a berserk animal in the cabin, or having to keep Chinky shut up which he would have hated.

Chinky wore his disdainful expression. He had his own label and his own ticket. He knew how to behave. He was a superior cat, an oriental, a warrior, athlete, supernatural being, and now a sophisticated traveller.

The sophisticated traveller bit the memsahib's sister on the leg in Calcutta. He did not care for Calcutta. It smelt different; the poverty rose in a wave and hit his delicate sense of smell, used to the scent of fish and the moist green aromatics of his beloved tea country.

Calcutta was an endless pageant of peasants, bearded Sikhs, holy men and sacred cows, cars, bicycles, buffalo and rickshaws, oxcarts, trucks, taxis and beggars. It was groaning with the burden of its growing population; an astonishing, overwhelmingly noisy place, palled with factory smoke, the din of steamer whistles invading even the human clamour.

The memsahib stayed in Calcutta for fourteen days and dared not let Chinky off his lead. That was why he bit her sister's leg.

He was sorry afterwards. But it was too late to make amends. He breathed a sigh of relief when they took off again for the long flight to Rome. There were several refuelling stops and comfort stations for Chinky. They rushed him to any available plant pot or patch of desert; this was fun. Chinky enjoyed the challenge. He often spotted a dry plant or dusty digging bowl first.

The apogee of the flight was when he was taken on his lead up to the flight deck to meet the pilot. He behaved as if he was always being taken to flight decks. It was all a bit of a mystery but he showed a polite interest in the dials and little flashing lights and everyone thought he was wonderful. Which he was.

The weekend stop in Rome presented a few problems. They left an indignant Chinky locked in the hotel bedroom, and hung up the DO NOT DISTURB notice. He was furious. He wanted to explore. Later they took him for a walk on his lead. He guessed it was a new version of spot the plant, and instead found a drain in a cleaning room.

Chinky was intrigued by the view of London from the air but not so keen on Heathrow. An airport policeman and a man from the quarantine kennels boxed up the spitting Siamese warrior and took him away in a van.

The memsahib watched them take Chinky away. She wondered sadly how he would cope with confinement. He had always been so free.

'This is not just an ordinary cat,' said the vet examining Chinky at the kennels. 'This is a strong character, a very strong character indeed.'

Chinky glared at him, blue eyes gleaming, long cream tail whipping the air. He was straining with frustration and fury.

'You are perhaps a little too fierce for domestic life in England. No tigers to fight here, old chap.'

After being neutered, Chinky was one degree easier to cope with; he became companionable and affectionate, but only with the very few people he liked. To the rest of the world his attitude was exactly the same.

He settled to life in England but there were no snakes to catch, no rumbling or roaring in the night or beating of the drums. His paws itched to be off, and an hour after being let out of quarantine, he was off up a tree, the memsahib hanging onto his lead. Time passed and his fur darkened that first winter in England. When a special hutch arrived he had no idea that he was about to embark on the biggest adventure of all.

The SS *Uganda* left Tilbury early at dawn one morning in October 1957. Chinky was more than a little puzzled at his new quarters in the hutch secured on one of the forward decks. The train journey to the docks had been invigorating, looking out of windows and watching the rural countryside flashing by, but now this new place . . . a house on water? Chinky was cautious, reserving his options.

He soon made it quite clear, and loudly, that he had no intention of staying put in his hutch. Once the ship had passed through the Bay of Biscay, he was indignantly asking to be let out. He was not going to spend the entire voyage cooped up like some pathetic invalid when there were so many new things to see and smell.

He got very bad tempered, and when the purser put his hand into the cage uninvited, Chinky bit his finger. It was a protest on behalf of all hutch-haters.

'I suppose I'll have to take you out on your lead just to keep you quiet,' said the memsahib. Chinky stood patiently while she fixed his lead to the collar. 'Now don't let me down. Behave.'

Chinky smirked his Siamese smirk. It was not quite a grin. He knew how to behave. Hadn't he been trained? He took to the ship like a second home; he had four sea legs in no time. He went everywhere. Everyone knew him. He was someone. But the swimming pool puzzled him; he could see no point in people splashing about in that horrid wet stuff.

It began to get very hot in the Red Sea. He lay panting in the hutch, his fur like an extra heated blanket wrapped round his skin. It had been hot in Assam, but the breeze from the jungle hills had tempered the air.

The memsahib was worried. She spent a lot of time on her knees talking to him and taking him cool water to drink. She took him to her cabin, where he lay under a damp cloth. Perhaps she should have left Chinky in England – but who would have given a home to a half-wild Siamese? Who would have loved him? No, she had done the right thing bringing Chinky with them to Kenya, but at the moment it was far too hot for someone wearing a permanent fur coat.

The captain came to the rescue.

'It's far too hot here for that animal,' he said, stating the obvious. 'Move the hutch up to my deck where there's more breeze.'

Chinky spent the rest of the voyage on the captain's deck, which was, of course, his rightful place. He could have told them that.

Chinky had a splendid view of Fort Jesus, which commands the entrance channel to Mombasa harbour. Mombasa was built on an island, a coral atoll, with deep water north and south. He could see the old harbour with ancient curved dhows at anchor, the dense mass of Arab houses, and ahead the modern city that had sprung up with the port of Kilindini.

The cat was tense with barely contained excitement. This was a totally new place! They went over the causeway linking the island to mainland, past many-storeyed houses jammed together in narrow streets thronged with black-skinned people.

They began the 320-mile train journey to Nairobi, climbing through the coastal hills, then the long haul over undulating country, speeding through cuttings and embankments some over forty-five feet high. Chinky was convinced they were travelling inside mountains.

The memsahib scratched under his smooth brown chin as he darted this way and that, taking in all the new sights.

'Soon be there,' she said wearily. 'Not long now.'

Chinky could sleep. He could sleep anywhere. But the memsahib slept only fitfully, keeping half an eye open on Chinky and their luggage.

They crossed dry and scorched plains dancing with dust devils in the shimmering heat, another source of astonishment to the cat.

They drove along the main avenue in the capital city, a wide handsome road built so that a trek cart drawn by sixteen oxen could turn completely. Now there were new office blocks, hotels and shops shining in the harsh sunlight, each street a profusion of trees and flowers, jacarandas carpeting the ground with blue blossom, fountains of bougainvillaea spilling from balconies.

Chinky liked everything about Nairobi except the anti-rabies injection which he had to have before they journeyed further up-country. He spat and scratched the veterinary assistants, but it was no good. This was wild-animal country and one small brown and cream cat was no problem.

They soon left behind the gardened highway of the city and took to the unmade earth roads that crossed the Great Rift Valley. The weather-eroded grassland was dotted with acacia thorn trees and bushes, lakes where massed pink flamingoes strutted, and zebra and wildebeeste grazing the dry grasses. Chinky saw buck and gazelle, heard hyenas, smelt leopard and lion, screeched back at the chattering monkeys swinging in the trees.

Chinky settled quickly to living in several bungalows, travelling everywhere with them to various tea gardens in up-country Kenya, picnicking with the family in the beautiful green and uncultivated country of the Nandi Hill district, where the tea plantations were just beginning to be planted out. It was a lovely land of green rolling hills and deep valleys, cultivated farms and native *shambas* with round thatched huts and sweet corn growing close by.

Chinky would still not tolerate any other animals except their own labrador, and even chased off a long-nosed ant-eater who ventured onto the veranda. The astonished creature had never faced a wild, spitting, arched-back Siamese warrior before. He took to his heels, leaving Chinky victorious.

It was possibly an insect that nearly killed Chinky. Suddenly he became so ill that the memsahib took him fifty miles to the nearest vet. Sickness and weakness made Chinky no more docile and the vet had difficulty handling him.

'I've no suitable drugs here,' he said despairingly. He could see the cat was going downhill fast. A raging fever clouded the intelligent blue eyes.

The memsahib took him home, cradled in his basket from Assam, stopping frequently to feed him milk and brandy from a dropper. It was one journey that Chinky never wanted to experience again.

Back home, he spent the days lying on the memsahib's lap or crouching in a cool spot by the bungalow's shade. He gradually recovered; he was never quite the same warrior, although the fierce spirit was still there.

Two crested cranes decided to live in the field next to their garden. Chinky did not like this at all. He did not want the two big proud birds living so close to him. He started to stalk them, crouching in the long grass, a low growl coming from his throat.

But the big birds were not afraid of one small cat. They began to dance round him, their great black and white wings outspread menacingly. Chinky stood his ground, spitting and hissing with his squashed hat look. He countered their attack with aggressive yowls, fur standing on end . . .

Suddenly Chinky lost his nerve, raced back to the fence and fled to the safety of the garden. He was trembling, but not with fear. He was furious with himself. He had met his match and it was difficult to accept.

Three years later Chinky undertook his last long journey, the flight home to England. The regulations had changed and Chinky was not allowed to travel with the family. He boarded a special animal freight plane in a specially constructed crate. The memsahib was apprehensive, but what could she do? She could not argue with an international airline that Chinky was a seasoned traveller and better behaved than most.

No one knew what Chinky went through on that flight or what strange animal cries came from the other crates . . . wildebeeste, monkeys, lions . . . perhaps even an elephant. If he was terrified he did not show it. But when they visited him in quarantine in Folkestone, he got so over-excited because he thought he was being taken out, they decided it was not fair to visit him again until it was time to take him home.

It was a long six months. But Chinky did not forget them. He was overjoyed to see the memsahib again. They put on his collar and lead and he leaped without hesitation into the car. Thank goodness that's over, his look said. Where are we going now? But this time he was not going far.

His new home was a long sunny garden in Sussex, down a quiet lane shaded with leafy trees. He still defended his territory, but now there were only squirrels to chase off the strawberry beds and birds and butterflies and ants that scuttled over the warm paving stones. He missed the old adventures but he did not complain. He knew he was slowing down and memories of his great journeys were growing dim. He was content to sit and doze in the dappled afternoon sun and dream of his warrior days, occasionally whipping his long tail . . . still proud and fierce.

Give or take a few ship's cats, Chinky knew he must be the most travelled cat in the world: ten thousand miles or more with not a hair out of place. He yawned. It must be some sort of record . . .

Chinky died, aged eighteen, in his old cane basket from Assam.

Cat Knievel

No one told me there was going to be an audition. Nor that I was the item being auditioned. How was I to know, as I munched my way through a man-sized breakfast, that today I was required to look sleek and athletic, and not like an over-stuffed ginger-banded bean bag?

I was aware of the air of tension in the kitchen as I polished off the leftovers in Hebe's bowl. Hebe is a black Persian queen with an appetite like a bird, which is just as well for me. I took me and my stomach to the windowsill for a tidy-up while I had the strength. My fawn paws worked overtime as I coaxed my thick russet and caramel fur into near perfect order.

'I must have been mad,' Val was saying, rushing around cleaning up the place. This meant we were having visitors. I knew the signs. 'I wish I'd never written to them. After all, I mean, what does it matter, really?'

'You knew they'd go for it,' said Robert. 'It's just the kind of thing they love. A performing cat and an idiot owner. They don't often get both at once.'

'I'm going to look a fool if Copper won't cooperate,' Val wailed. 'He'll probably sleep all afternoon and refuse to budge an inch. Oh no, we've run out of cat sweets. I'll have to rush to the shops and get some. He'll never perform without his usual bribe.'

'Bribe?'

'Reward.'

By now I had the faintest suspicion that they were talking about me partly because my name is Copper and I am addicted to cat sweeties. I need my daily fix. Sorry, folks, that's just a joke. I'm doing what comes naturally, and if a little reward comes my way naturally too, then I'm not one to refuse.

'May I point out that Evel Knievel is at present looking so unhealthily fat that I doubt if he could jump over a pincushion if you gave him a hefty push,' said Robert as he left for work.

Val scooped me up into her arms. I purred hello, patted her face gently, tugged a claw through a tempting brown curl.

'He weighs a ton,' she said, her voice doom-laden. 'He won't be able to do a thing.'

That was true. I only felt like sleeping it off under my favourite forsythia bush at the end of the garden.

A young man arrived, sleek, smooth, trendy. I could tell from his voice that he was not over the moon about cats. His name was Martin O'Connell and he was a director. Director of what? But I was only marginally curious.

'Do you like cats?' I heard Val asking him.

'I can take them or leave them,' he replied, with a distinct lack of enthusiasm.

I settled back into the warm crushed grass of my hideaway. It was nothing to do with me. The pale March sunshine dappled my coppery fur and lulled me into an unsuspecting doze.

But suddenly it had a great deal to do with me. I was unceremoniously heaved out and cajoled into my routine. It was the same old stuff – sit, beg, lie down, shake hands. Years ago, for reasons she cannot remember, Val had decided to train me in basic obedience as one would a dog. I was very easy to teach, of course, being intelligent and an extrovert. I didn't mind the treats either.

'Paw.'

I held out my left paw. Always my left. It's something to do with balance.

'Down.'

I flopped down, full length. I went through it all, trying to maintain a matching lack of enthusiasm, reacting to Val's voice and hand signals with an air of casual sophistication. I was doing it all for Val, though I do quite enjoy it. The O'Connell man was looking at me without any expression. I could do that too. I stared back at him, unflinching. I do have the strangest colour eyes; they are the colour of the underside of a new leaf, like the clear green sea off Cyprus; like a piece of polished green onyx marble in a museum. They can be disconcerting to some humans.

'Well . . . how about this jumping over toddlers you say he can do,' the director went on, continuing his laid-back attitude.

'Yes, yes,' said Val, rapidly producing our own home-grown toddler, a two-year-old variety called Jenni, and a collection of toys to add to the line-up.

'Jump,' Val commanded.

I cleared toddler and teddy with one spring. I was certainly not at my best as I was carrying a lot of extra weight. But Mr O'Connell seemed marginally impressed.

'Could we add a few more toddlers?' he suggested.

For two hours I defied gravity, heaving my great bulk over various toddlers and objects. Not satisfied with toddler-jumping, the director wanted to see stunning feats of athleticism involving various toys and children.

'Could we get him to jump over a toddler pushing a pram?' suggested Martin with signs of interest glimmering in his eyes. 'What do you think, eh?'

Val looked at me dubiously. It had been half-day

closing at the shops so she was rewarding me with biscuits, most of which I politely declined. She could see that I was getting tired and bored.

'I could get some more toddlers tomorrow,' she said, frantically thinking of her friends' offspring.

Martin went into a deep directorial think. I began to slink off. There was a limit to what I would do for a biscuit.

'Okay, then. We'll call it a day. The filming will begin at ten o'clock tomorrow. Sharp.'

They let me sleep on their bed. This was a great treat and I spent the night happily tramping about, pawing, clawing, purring, first with one and then the other. Of course, I did sleep but I can purr quite loudly even when fast asleep.

'Get this cat off the bed,' grumbled Robert from under the covers.

'No, I want Copper in a certain frame of mind for tomorrow,' said Val, trying to sleep with me half sprawled over her pillow, my fur tickling her nose. 'I want Copper to be relaxed and happy.'

'Urrgh . . . tomorrow.'

Anyone would think they didn't sleep well. I don't know what they were grumbling about; they've got a lovely bed. Try sleeping in a cardboard box in the kitchen every night and see how they'd like that.

'Will you go out and buy a bribe, I mean, a chicken,' asked Val anxiously at breakfast time. 'I'd like to cook it before the film crew arrive. It's for Copper's lunch.'

Lunch? Whatever happened to breakfast? I wolfed down the meagre spoonful of Whiskas on my saucer and looked up expectantly. What was that? A sample?

'Sorry, Copper. No more breakfast for you. This is your great day. You've got to be a little peckish.'

Peckish! I was starving. I prowled around, wondering what I could find that was edible. Crumbs from under the high-chair? There were some congealed bits of boiled egg and soggy cereal. No, thank you. Whatever was going on? Overfed one day, diet the next. I looked for the Persian queen's dish but it had been whisked away. Now that wasn't playing fair.

Okay then, don't feed me, I thought. They'd be sorry. I sat aloof, grooming my whiskers and long striped tail as if I didn't care. I was looking thinner already.

Suddenly the place erupted as the film crew arrived. There were hundreds of them, at least seven. I fled, watching the commotion from a safe distance. Furniture was moved out into the garden (were the family going to live in the garden? What about rain?); tall things with white faces were installed throwing out a bright hot glare. Long black snakes slithered around the living-room floor and boxes of equipment filled every available space.

Spotlights, cables, cameras, microphones . . . I'd never heard these strange words before. And the noise! The house was full of people all talking to each other at once and stomping about. What on earth was happening? I looked at Val, but she too had caught this distraught look.

People were stepping over other people as a man fiddled with something in the hall; another wrestled with a stubborn camera in the kitchen. The house had gone mad. It was like a rabbit warren on a Bank Holiday.

I kept out of the way though my nose was twitching with curiosity. The director arrived wearing a rakish cap and carrying a clipboard of notes. He was telling every-one else what to do. My poor stomach was rumbling. I connected Val's breakfast lapse with this horde of people who had invaded our house. I slid off into the garden. They wouldn't miss me. Perhaps they wouldn't even notice my disappearance for days . . .

'Where's Copper?' asked Val.

Her voice was like a thin reed in the lull before a storm.

There was a stunned silence. No one moved. The director went white. Panic swept through the assembled crew. Even the cables twitched. They were ready to film and the star had vanished.

'Oh my God. The cat,' gasped Martin. 'Find the cat. Esther will be furious.'

The whisper went round like a word game . . . find the cat, find the cat . . . careful now, don't scare him.

'Ah, there he is,' said Val with the air of a magician. 'I've spotted his ginger fur in the bushes.'

I was brought back, limp, disinterested, but I was only pretending. I could smell chicken cooking in the kitchen. That was a good sign.

The equipment and lights had been positioned. There were a lot of extra toddlers and every imaginable kind of toy. Were we having a jumble sale? Perhaps we had become a nursery school?

'Now, Copper darling,' said Val, taking me aside. 'This is your great chance. You're going to be famous. You're going to be on *That's Life*! Isn't that exciting?'

I nudged her chin. *That's Life*? Never heard of it. What was it, for heaven's sake? I'd been on a windowsill, on the top of a car, on a flower bed, but I'd never been on a that's life.

For the next six hours they had me working like a horse. Sit, beg, lie down, shake hands, jump this, jump that. Every conceivable camera angle was trained on me and caught on film.

Jumping toddlers isn't that easy. They move . . . unexpectedly. An arm, a leg, and curly little head can suddenly catch me in mid-flight. Ouch. It requires precision, timing and a certain expertise to cope with toddlers. I'm no amateur.

Someone crawled on the floor with this black object called a microphone and put it in front of my mouth. They wanted to catch me purring. I shook out my back leg. It's what I do when I'm embarrassed, and my goodness, was I embarrassed. It was covered in dust too. I gave it a quick lick. Then they wanted to catch me cleaning myself. Invasion of privacy, I called it. But I didn't complain. Val was rewarding me with masses of chicken morsels and I could handle quite a few.

There was a break for lunch; it was hardly worth my putting in an appearance. I got a kitten-size helping of chicken. What was going on? No proper meals but rewards coming my way like it was Christmas. Not the balanced diet I was accustomed to. Val wasn't eating much either.

Martin O'Connell was no longer so laid-back and remote. He became fired with enthusiasm for new stunts. He invented more complicated obstacles for me to jump over . . . toddler pushing pram, toddler on rocking horse, a two-storey green-tiled dolls' house, rows and rows of squirming toddlers side by side on the carpet . . . I was beginning to see toddlers coming out of the wall.

'Wonderful! Wonderful!' exclaimed Martin. 'Come on, Copper, you can do it! That's my baby! Did you catch that expression on film? I want that lion look. Again! Copper baby, you're the tops!'

By now I was like a machine, a gleaming oiled machine of muscles and sinews, my russet fur glowing in patches and stripes like fire under the hot lights. I leaped through the air, effortlessly and gracefully, my long tail streaming, a powerful beast of the jungle, a leopard in flight, muscles rippling under the taut shining coat. I was ecstatic. I could jump forever and I could jump anything. I could jump over trees, clear the roof tops, take on the moon . . .

One evening they insisted that I came indoors to watch some programme on television. Val and Robert were eagerly waiting to see what would be shown of six hours of filming. It had been weeks ago, way back in March. I'd almost forgotten all about it.

The programme began. We waited. I yawned delicately and wondered if I could ask to go out. There was far more going on in the garden.

'And now to Copper,' said Esther Rantzen, grinning widely. 'Our pet of the week. The toddler-leaping cat!'

'Jump!'

I pricked my ears. I heard Val's voice giving me my command. What did she want me to jump? But she was chatting away to Robert, not even looking at me.

'Jump!'

Hang on, now. She was doing it without moving her lips. I sat up, prepared to jump but the command simply wasn't clear. Jump what? The Sunday newspaper on the carpet . . .?

My attention was directed to the television screen. I yawned again. I hardly recognised the splodge of ginger doing all those pathetic little stunts. You should see me now. Since then I have gone on to perfecting bigger and better jumps. Now I am magnificent.

That other stuff was child's play.

Susie's Letters

Dear Auntie Joan,

You are so very good to me! You sent me my first real live letter – a true message of sympathy for my lost love – and then you made a special journey to see me and to bring me a gift of Mr Safeway's rabbit. It was delicious, thank you.

How can I ever make amends for my behaviour yesterday? I do love you, but please let me explain. The day began badly. I made my call to the garden much earlier than usual so that I would be ready for you, but I stopped to speak to two men delivering coal. How did I know that they were going to pat me? My white ruffle was black!

Mother grumbled and helped to remove some of the coal dust from my fur but I was disturbed by the incident. However, when you arrived, it was lovely. I was looking forward to being alone with you for a cosy chat in the afternoon. That's why I went into the garden while you had a peaceful lunchtime. And then! I got ambushed by two black and white cats for hours. They wouldn't let me move until you came out into the garden and then they chased me. Since Nelson went out of my life I have had

137

no wish for further male friends. I hope I made that clear.

As you say, males are too fickle, especially when a puss like that flapper Snowy winks at them. She is only two and I am nine years of age, but let Nelson find out for himself that youth can be very deceiving.

Speaking of age, I want to tell you about the deep sadness of my life. The first human friend I had was Isabelle. She was ninety-nine and very poor. She had one armchair and a bed in the same room and she always let me choose which I fancied for my afternoon rest. Part of her pension was put into a box and saved to buy me a tin of best salmon or sardines. When my mother heard of it, she said she was ashamed of me, but Isabelle and I understood each other. She said I was the loveliest thing in her life.

She died. Mother said that a lady of ninety-nine was too old to live. I do not understand that; she was so young in heart and mind. I grieved for her for months, sitting on her windowsill every day.

My next friend was Daisy, a lady of ninety-three years. I did not often go into her house, because she was afraid of my getting under her feet. I went to her back door to chat to her, caught all the mice from her falling down coalshed, and every sunny afternoon I waited in the garden until she brought her chair. She would nurse me and we would spend the afternoon in sleep. We were good friends, and I mourn her too.

My last friend was Mr M., who lives across the road. Regularly he would be at home for a day to clean and mend his car. I spent the day with him. If it was warm, I sat on top of the car, but if it was cold and damp, I sat inside and we chatted through the window. When there was a shower of rain, he would come inside and sit with me. That was very cosy. He would say in his kind, gruff voice: 'Poor little Susan'. You can tell that he understood me.

One day he told me he was going to retire and that we would have many days together. Soon afterwards I ran across the road to him but two men were holding him. He had died of a heart attack. What sorrow.

My mother is sorry for me and does all she can to make up for the loss of my loyal friends, but you can see, Auntie Joan, how I need your love, and I shall always be your most affectionate puss-niece,

Susan

PS   Having scorned Nelson on one occasion, I relented today and spent four hours with him. But no kissing! When he came this morning, he looked thin, dirty and miserable with a lump out of his tail. My heart melted and so did Mother's, for she gave him a piece of chicken. Whether the friendship will continue, I do not know, but he seemed comforted in sitting with me, and that's what love is all about, isn't it?

Mitcham
20 April 1980

Dear Auntie Joan,

Another little letter to you because my 'affair' with Nelson and then the altercation with him made me forget to answer the most important part of your letter to me.

Thank you for your kind invitation. I would love to see you and meet your beloved puss-cat Kiwi, but I think that the journey is too long for me. Perhaps it is a law of nature that humans cannot chose friends for their cats. My mother learned that lesson the hard way.

Thinking that we would all have a cosy Christmas afternoon together, she carried me round to her friend Mildred, who has two cats, Nimmo (he bears a remarkable resemblance to the actor Derek Nimmo) and Sookie. It was a disaster!

Nimmo pranced around with back arched like a silly tom-cat and Sookie rushed behind a door and kept peeking out at me. How would you feel, Auntie, if Uncle Wally took you to a strange house for tea, and someone ran behind a door and peeped out at you? I was very disturbed and so I sat on a chair and swore continuously on one note, scarcely pausing for breath, until I was wrapped in a blanket and taken home again to spend the rest of the afternoon alone. I needed that solitude to regain my equilibrium.

My mother tells me that your surname is 'Toy'. What a lovely name. (I adore my toys, especially Sally and Tommy, whom I suckle or kick according to my mood.) What better name could you have? My only other choice for you would be 'Rabbit' or perhaps 'Smoked Haddock'. Not so special as Toy, but two of my favourite dishes.

Nelson is still poorly, with a lump out of his tail. It looks very sore. Mother would like to take him to the vet to have his health checked and then adopt him – but I say no, very firmly. The pangs of jealousy would be too great for me to bear, Auntie, and I would have to leave home.

The other black and white male is still trying to force his charm upon me and the other night upset me deeply. Being put to bed is a personal and intimate occasion. I am cuddled and lowered gently into my basket and left with a kiss and a little prayer. That old moggy sat the other side of the door and listened! How rude and insensitive can you get? He is a good-looking, dapper little fellow. Just the type that you can never trust.

When I write next, Auntie, I would like to tell you about my early life. It began very happily but did not progress according to plan. In my case, my foster-mother had to become my mother, and I lost a whole family at one blow. But that is a long story and will take at least two letters to relate.

All my love and purr-rr-rr's to you,
from your puss-niece
Susan

Mitcham
Written from my favourite
chair in the sitting room

Dear Auntie Joan,

I am writing to tell you that for a few days I have been a very sad puss. My little human girl friend, Jane, took me to her home just round the corner, and there in a garden I saw my one-eyed Nelson kiss Snowy, a pure-white coated cat. (There is nothing else pure about her.) She is a pert little flirt but my Nelson has yet to find out how worthless she is.

Of course, I am not so broken-hearted as I was over my first and real love, Tibby-Tabs. We spent part of every day together and, when I was ill, he visited me twice a day and watched me through the window. I lost him three years ago from an attack of 'flu.

My only companions now are Tom and Jerry – two growing kittens who live two doors away. I hate them. You may remember that I had a ginger neighbour, Freddie, who disappeared one evening. He was my hero and taught me three things – to swear, to spit and a third device which is too indecent to mention to you (you will be pleased to know that I have dropped all use of it). I employ the first two skills to keep those conceited kittens in their place.

All my purr-purrs,
Ever your loving
Susie

Mitcham
10 May 1980

Dear Auntie Joan Toy,

Thank you for your letter. I am indeed lucky to have such a devoted auntie, and although I like Mr Purr, the butcher, I still think that Toy is *the* most wonderful name.

Thank you also for the cake that you sent home on my

141

mother's last visit to you. Did you know that I like your cakes? It has to be your own make, of course.

On Wednesday mornings a lady named Ruby comes to help us, and this time Mother gave her a piece of your cake. I *made* her share it with me. I know it is not good manners but the scent of the cake is so delicious that I cannot resist pushing and scratching until I am given a share.

Yes, Auntie, I do think that cats have 'nine lives'. It is because we are very wise and we can act quickly and cleverly in most difficult circumstances. Also we are shrewd in judging human character and we soon learn whom we can trust – and ways of watching cruel or careless people. Of course, we vary in character and intelligence, as you know, but given reasonable care, I am proud to say that our brains are superb and we know how to use them.

In my last letter I said that my life had not developed as planned. I will now begin to tell my story.

My mother was a lovely little puss called Mina. She had only one eye (perhaps that is why I like Nelson) but she was the best mother a kitten could have, and she taught me my good manners. One day she told me and my brothers that it was time for us to think about leaving her and making our own way in the world. We all cried but she told us to be brave, because her human mother was kind and would try to find us happy homes.

That afternoon a gentleman named Mike arrived with a little girl, Sharon. He chose one of my brothers, but Sharon held on to me and would not let me go. She pleaded with her daddy until he agreed that I should be taken to their home. It was a long journey. I had never been in a car and I clung to Sharon and cried all the way.

When we arrived home, I found a lovely human mother, Pat, and another little girl, Michelle. They all made a great fuss of me – I was very pretty with a little kitten body and a beautiful fluffy tail. I was so happy, Auntie. They let me do just as I liked and I slept with

Sharon every night, until I found out that Mike danced professionally and did not come home some nights until two o'clock in the morning.

I used to hide in the bushes when I was called in the evening and play in the street until Mike came home. We would sleep together downstairs so that we did not disturb the family upstairs.

When I was about a year old, a puppy named Brandy joined the family. He was great fun and we chased each other round the house in the day and sometimes in the night until Mike shouted at us to be quiet. Then others joined the family – a parrot (I never spoke to him), rabbits, chickens and lots of pigeons. I can never understand that human phrase 'put the cat amongst the pigeons'. I was always with them and the rabbits and the chickens. We all played together and nothing ever happened to us.

There was one incident, but it was not my fault. Little Flora Fantail was one of Mike's special favourites but she was a dim-witted pigeon. She fell down the chimney of my present mother's house along the road and got herself stuck on a ledge. Fred, the ginger cat, and I rushed into the house, sat either side of the fireplace and talked to her. She answered but would not come down. All the neighbours tried to help.

On the third day, the RSPCA inspector arrived. He called the fire brigade, but they could not get old fantail. The next day he called an old-fashioned sweep. A little old man came with brushes and rods and fixed them up the chimney. Nothing happened!

We thought Flora had died, but just as we were all having a sooty cup of tea (sooty milk for Fred and me), she hopped onto the brush and was rescued with a lot more soot. She was quite composed and haughty, as if it was her usual habit to sit in chimneys. Mike gave her away to a gentleman living in the country, but she refused to stay and came back to sit on the chimney. How could anyone be so dim?

There was one other happening. Old Robert Pigeon fell down my friend Daisy's chimney. She was frightened and would not let me in. I had to watch everything through the window. My present foster-mother called the emergency gas officer to unfix the gas fire, and there was Rob in the grate. He was looking very poorly so she put him in her bath. She intended to give him a little brandy, but her hand slipped and she gave him a whole spoonful. She thought she had killed him, but no, he was quite drunk and snored all night in the bath. In the morning, Mike cleaned him and put the broken leg in a splint, and as far as I know he is still living.

Lots of loving purrs,
your puss-niece
Susan

Mitcham
27 May 1980

Dear Auntie Joan Toy,

Another piece of your special puss cake! How clever of you to know the exact number of currants I like in each portion. Do you think of me as you count them into the cooking bowl?

I thought today that from the cosiness of my mother's bed (my special cover is on it, of course), I would continue my memoirs.

When I was two and half years of age, Mike took me aside and explained to me that he was what humans call 'black'. (I had not noticed any difference because I too am mainly black.) He said that he had a dear mother far away across the sea and she would like to see him. He could not take any animals, so would I live with a foster-mother for five weeks? What could I say, Auntie? After a little cry, I agreed, because I knew the lady who was to be my foster-mother.

The day of departure came. I was carried along to house number sixteen from house number ten, and put into the arms of my foster-mother. Auntie, my life changed suddenly. I had to learn a new word: 'discipline'. No running round the streets at night, or hiding in the bushes till 2 a.m., eating and sleeping where I liked. No! I could play in the street until 9 p.m., but on the stroke of the clock I had to be indoors. After an hour of playing up and down the stairs, I was put to bed in my own basket in my own room and left with a goodnight kiss and a prayer for my safety while my family was away.

Sometimes my foster-mum would call out in the night: 'Are you all right, Susie?' and I would mee-ee-eeow: 'I'm lonely.' She would come and carry me back to bed with her for the rest of the night. That was lovely. She would have had me every night but, not being disciplined before, I wanted to play and have a snack in the middle of the night. It was too disturbing, she said.

Time passed pleasantly. The only trouble was Fred! We were supposed to share our foster-mother, but I soon learned that Fred never wanted to share anything. I tried every ruse and wile I knew. I tried creeping up and kissing him while he slept, but he would wake in a great fury and swear abominably. I chased him, played with him, scared him by hiding behind the curtains and doors. (I could hear my foster mother say: 'Careful, Fred. She's hiding somewhere.')

Nothing would coax him, and then one day, my patience exhausted, I terrified him. I chased him into the drain and held him there until my foster-mother found us . . . Fred crouched on the grating, and me sitting on the side above him with my paw raised menacingly. Fred was rescued and given some cream. I was scolded and slapped, and after that we ignored each other. If we met accidentally, we passed with a spit and a hiss, until the day, years later, Fred disappeared. I will tell you that story another time.

After a long, long time my family returned and everyone came along to carry me home to number ten. We hugged and kissed each other. Brandy and I rushed around the house madly. All discipline was forgotten (except Mike noticed how well-behaved I was at first), and life was normal and happy again. I thought forever, but it was not to be.

All my purrs, dear Auntie,
Your loving puss-niece,
Susan

Mitcham
June 1980

Dear Auntie Joan Toy,

I am continuing my memoirs quickly, because I have a puss foreboding that something is going to happen in my life. A change that makes my spine quiver and my tail twitch.

Pat, my human mother, was always looking after the children, feeding them, putting them to bed, getting them up again, and bathing them. We kittens were taught to attend to ourselves at a very early age, but I did have an unexpected human bath once.

My foster-mother has a bathroom downstairs. She leaves the window open and by jumping onto the shed (it is my shed, with a cat door and a basket in case I get caught out in the rain), I can fix my back feet onto the window frame, slide my front paws half way down the bathroom wall, and then make a clever leap and land between the bath and the toilet seat. I then curl up on the mat until the door is opened and she says: 'Hello, come in, Susie.'

One particular afternoon, I was just about to follow this procedure, then to my surprise I saw her in the bath. Her warning: 'Careful Susie, the wall is wet' was too late. My front paws slid too far and I somersaulted into the bath with my foster-mother. What a splash! There was I, soaking wet, sitting on her tummy. Before you could say 'tails and whiskers', I was wrapped in one towel and she was wrapped in another, sitting in front of the fire trying to dry ourselves. I had hot milk whilst she had hot tea and we were none the worse for our adventure.

The only other time that I had a bath was very unfortunate. My foster-mother has a goldfish pond at the bottom of her garden. Fred spends hours on the side and sometimes he catches a fish, which he brings over as a gift to my foster-mother. (She never looks very pleased.) One day I thought I would try fishing. I sat there patiently for a long time, and then Fred must have crept up behind me because all of a sudden I felt a paw on my back. I lost my balance and felt myself drowning. Freddie sat there smirking, whiskers twitching, while I scrambled out and rushed in to my foster-mother. Once more I was wrapped in a towel and given hot milk, but she would not believe that Freddie had pushed me. She said that she did not listen to such tales, and so he never had the scolding he deserved.

But, dear Auntie Joan, then something really dreadful happened to me. The family found another house, not far away, and Mike said that it would not be safe to take me. I would have to live with my foster-mother always and not keep visiting from one home to the other. I cried and cried, but it all came to pass. Life was never the same. I used to sit on the windowsill of my old home, just hoping, but my foster-mother would come along and cuddle me and carry me home. So I had to learn to accept her as my mother. She told me that the only place my surname would be changed was on my sick record card at the vet's.

Next time, dear Auntie, I will tell you what happened in my new life.

> All my purr-purrs for a little while,
> from your puss-niece,
> Susan

Dear Auntie Joan Toy,

Sometimes I too get a poorly head and I am so sorry for you. I wonder if you bang yours against the wardrobe as I do. Some of our furniture stands on polished lino and I love to chase a ball around the bedroom, but I go so fast I cannot stop myself, then bang! that's my head hit something. A dangerous game, Auntie. Please do not play it too often, because it will worry my mother if she knows that both of us have a sore head.

When Freddie knew that I was going to live here, there were terrible scenes. His temper was uncontrollable and his language unprintable! He came to meals as usual but would not share my place-mat. He insisted on having his meals on top of the fridge and then sleeping on the plate-rack of the cooker.

One night I thought that I would try sleeping on the plate-rack. It was exciting. You could stand up and look into the kitchen next door. When Fred came in for breakfast, I thought he was going to explode!

He spent quite a lot of time under the bed too. Mother and I would pop upstairs and take him a little cream.

She would say: 'Never mind, Susie. He can't help it.' She was upset really, Auntie, and felt that her house had been taken over by two uncivilised cats.

Occasionally we would make a pact to give up washing ourselves for a week, or hide at night when we were called then ask for the door to be opened about 4 a.m. This was life for the next two years.

Then one foggy October evening, Fred disappeared. When Mother called us, the fog was very thick and Fred did not come. He never missed a meal and we knew that something was wrong. All the children in the neighbourhood joined in the search. For weeks the postman, the milkman, the window cleaner and everyone looked for him, but he was never seen again. Poor dear Fred! We cried for him.

I missed my own dear family very much. How much I did not know myself until later that year. My next letter will tell you.

My love and purr-rrs,
Your puss-niece,
Susan

Mitcham
June 1980

My dear Auntie Joan Toy,

A sad little puss-niece is writing to you today because my old home at number ten is empty again and I cannot get in to look in all the corners. No one knows why I go to all the corners. It is a secret that I keep to my own puss-self.

After that, all the cats of the neighbourhood came to sympathise with me. Then my life became very peaceful. I played in the garden with the children next door. They shared their sweets with me until I was sick.

One night I was naughty and stayed out with my own special puss, Tibby-Tabs. He had a bad cold and the first thing I did when I went into breakfast was to sneeze. Mother was upset and gave me some cod-liver oil and malt, but it was no good. I was ill and had to go twice to the vet.

Tibby-Tabs was not well and a week after that he died. I had a relapse and was very ill indeed. Mother kept me in my bed with a fire night and day. The vet gave me injections and pills, but I was just fading away.

One day Mother remembered how clever her friend Richard was and asked him to help. He understood and explained to her that I was not trying to get better. Although I knew that my old family loved me, when they left their home empty, I felt that I had been abandoned, and in my weakness, I had lost the will to live. Mother was distressed. She used to get up in the night

149

and tell me that I was loved and wanted. Then I would purr for her softly but I could not eat.

One morning I knew that I was fading away – the vet could do no more for me – and so Mother took my paw and kissed it. She said: 'All right, Susie, if you want to die, I'll let you go, and hold your paw.' Suddenly, Auntie, I knew that I could not leave her, and so I dragged myself to the edge of the basket and took a little milk and brandy. I began to get better from that moment.

The vet was so envious that I was being fed on chicken and jelly and cod in butter sauce, he said he would come and live with us when he was not well. I am glad that he did not come because I would not like to live with a man who was always taking my temperature and looking in my ears and mouth and feeling my tummy every day.

One winter evening I heard men's voices over the wall of some waste ground. It used to belong to the LEB, and then it was quite safe to visit the staff, to run up the fire escape of a stores building. After they left I was told never to go over the wall, but my curiosity got the better of me and that night I went to see what was happening.

The men got hold of me and put some nasty smelly stuff on my head and round my neck ruffle. Now one of my tricks is to lie very still and pretend I am not going to move, and then because I am double-jointed, I suddenly twist my body and I am off like a streak of lightning. I practise this trick on Mother sometimes.

My trick worked and I managed to get away and run home. Mother wrapped me in a towel and the next morning rushed me to the vet's. I had to stay in hospital for two days while I was cleaned and part of my ruffle was cut away. It was a terrifying experience, and please tell your own puss Kiwi about it so that she is warned. Sometimes men put this green thick liquid on you before they carry you off to be sold. Even in the few years that I have lived here, several cats have been lost for ever.

Mother has been in a search-party looking for them,

but she will never let me help. I am very carefully guarded when strangers are around. Only once I did get into the milkman's van and nearly got carried off to the depot, but he would have brought me back safely because he knew my name.

I will write soon and finish my memoirs, for I am wise and sensitive in my age, and I know that there is a great change coming to me for future years. I am sure that Mother would not let anything hurt me and so I must be happy and patient and await my new life.

With lots and lots of purrs,
from your puss-niece,
Susan

Mitcham
Still June 1980

My own dear Auntie Joan Toy,

Thank you for your loving letter. It was just what your puss-niece needed, for you have heard about my return to my family and the mixture of joy and sadness for me and my foster-mother.

A lady with a great big Airedale dog came to live at Number 10. He had a loud deep voice, especially when he saw me. I watched him at a safe distance every day, and then one day when my mother was out shopping, he broke down the fences, ploughed through the gardens (all the plants went flying into the air) and tried to attack me.

After that I was too frightened to ever go out again, even in the arms of my mother, who tried to comfort me and make me brave. My nerves were shattered. Nelson came regularly to see me. He sat on the kitchen window-sill and Mother would lift me up to kiss him and talk to him but I was afraid all the time.

My first mother, Pat, has been to see me and I am going back to live with her and Mike. Foster-mother has been doing my packing for me. Such a lot I have to take!

My basket, bed and rug, my bean-bag bed, which I like to use during the day, my brush and comb, my cat basket in case I have to go to the vet's, my toys, my night tray, my rabbit saucepan, my packet of biscuits, three tins of Whiskas and a bag of turkey-fido.

This is my last letter to you, dear Auntie, because I cannot write from my new address. I was four and a half years with my family, then four and a half years with my foster-mother, and I expect to be another four and a half years with my family again. My life has been turned into a complete circle, but that is not the end of me, Auntie. When cats just sit and gaze quietly, they are looking into eternity. My foster-mother knows that and talks to me about it. We all have to die, but there is no 'death' as humans sometimes think, for all life returns to God who gave it, so one day I will be with you again, dear Auntie.

Until then, all my purrs,
from your own dear puss-niece,
Susan

PS from Susan's foster-mother:

I would like to add 'Amen' to Susan's last letter. She is now happily settled in with her original family, behaving like the wanderer returned, demanding attention and generally taking command of the whole family.

I miss her intensely and shall for the rest of my life. There can never be another Susan. Thank you, Joan, for being her dear Auntie Joan Toy. (How she enjoyed your cake!)

Star Struck

The deputation waited at the end of the lane, vague shapes moving in the moonlight, as mist rolling up from the Thames enveloped them, obscuring their dimensions. They were not there by chance. They met her every night. They knew what they were doing.

As a car approached the lane, their yellow eyes lit up and glinted in the sudden light, jewel bright.

'Hello, my darlings,' she called. Excitement stirred through the group and they clustered round the car so that the driver could not go on. Then habit reasserted itself and Dimly, their leader, turned towards the cottage.

It was after midnight and ten plumes of tails waved in the headlights as the car proceeded at a cat's pace along the lane, the deputation leading the car and welcoming their mistress home.

For some people, perhaps, ten cats might seem to be a bit over the top. But for Beryl Reid it is as natural as breathing. She collects cats as other people collect certain china, brasses or seaside souvenirs. She has lost count of the number of cats there have been in her life, but she has not forgotten their names: the eccentric roof and bridge dweller Lulu; one-eyed Emma; gorgeous Georgie Girl, who lived for twenty years; childhood Jumbo and

...isn; beloved Footy, another twenty-year-old; Cuppy, a theatre cat who was more like a puppy following her around; the eighteen-pound Fred . . . They were shadows mingling with the current cats that wove around Beryl in the chilling river mist. No cat ever really left her. They stayed in her memory, long years after they had left this earth.

Dimly stretched his long black back and arched his spine. He was the only black among the current cats, who were predominantly ginger. There were four short-haired ginger cats, one long-haired ginger, one Olde English tortoiseshell, an enormous grey tabby and two brown tabbies. Dimly did a quick count. Did that make ten? He thought it did and yawned.

She was very late that evening. He had no idea where she went so regularly every day. She left at the same time in the afternoon and returned late in the dark. She was a night creature like them.

He did not know what being Beryl Reid meant. He understood nothing about theatres in London or her star billing. She was Queen Bee to him. It was the cats' name for her. Her father had called her Bee, which confirmed that the cats' choice was exactly right.

They were a motley crew. Bee's cats came from all walks of life.

Elsie was a nervous creature, unsure of how to behave after living with an Asian family in Bristol. She was acquired during a run of *Born in the Gardens* at the Theatre Royal. She was called Elsie because that was the name of the unseen cat featured in the play. But the real Elsie was a hell-cat.

Dimly was not around when Elsie first came to Honeypot Cottage, but he heard that she flew at Bee, clawing her legs till they bled. This went on for weeks until Bee said one day, in a voice that meant business: 'Elsie, how do you fancy a one-way trip to the vet's?'

Elsie did not know that Bee was an actress, nor that she would never have taken such a drastic step. But the threat worked. Elsie had a change of heart and became quite a push-over for affection.

Ronnie, at thirteen the oldest cat in the clan, was found by Bee dying of cat 'flu in a barn on a farm in Langley. Dimly had heard the story a hundred times.

She was in the country on location, filming *No Sex Please, We're British*, with Ronnie Corbett, when she discovered a tiny four-week-old kitten dying in a barn. A vet was on the set because there was a pig in the film, and Bee got him to have a look at the kitten. He said he would give it a 'flu injection and nine pills for Beryl to administer, but he did not hold out much hope.

'It won't live, you know,' he said.

'I really can't leave that little thing here,' she said.

The vet had not reckoned on Bee's determination. She got those nine pills down the tiny kitten and now Ronnie is a big butch cat, a beautiful golden-ginger colour with thick fluffy trousers.

She called him after her fellow actor, and every time she sees Ronnie Corbett, she tells him: 'Your child's doing very well.'

Dimly's own beginnings were through the RSPCA; he was one of an unwanted litter of three that arrived at the cottage on Bee's birthday in June. They became Sir Harry (named after Sir Harry Secombe), Muriel and Dimly. Sir Harry is a huge tabby with a penchant for children; Muriel is the Olde English and looks like a shaggy sheep; Dimly is the black-as-midnight cat.

Clive and Billy also came via the RSPCA and Bee has taught them to sit and stay. She believes that cats can be taught in the same way as dogs, though Barbara Woodhouse did not think this was possible.

The two newest kittens, Tufnell (called after one of Irene Handel's characters) and Paris (who slew Achilles and brought about the siege of Troy when he eloped with Helen), were also acquired from the RSPCA. Their staff thought of having a direct line to Honeypot Cottage.

The latest arrival is Jennie, a mature brown tabby in the

throes of cat grief. She had lived with an old lady who died, and was left without a home. Again the RSPCA knew who to ring for help; they knew who could coax a depressed puss back to the land of the living.

Dimly has no doubt about his Queen Bee's ability and vigour. She works hard, has dozens of engagements and little time off; she entertains and cooks wonderful meals for her friends; she also cooks for the cats – heart, liver, chicken and breast of lamb. She tries to remember which cat likes to eat what even though it is easy to get confused, especially the morning after a very late return home from the theatre.

He heard that she once fell in the river trying to rescue Footy. He was the cat who always tried to sit on her feet. He had strolled along the trunk of a willow tree, quite far out over the river. No one sitting in the garden actually saw the rescue operation, but the next minute Beryl appeared, soaked to the skin, pretty dress dripping, hair in rat's-tails, face streaming.

'I've fallen in the river,' she shrieked. 'My hair's like a Mars bar. And look at that cat!'

Footy was returning nonchalantly along the same branch. He sprang onto the lawn, unaware of all the fuss.

Bee is always saying that Dimly ought to have been called Brightly; he got his odd name in a very strange way. Some friends were staying at the cottage and looking for Beryl. One of them, Olivia, looked over to the carport and said: 'I think I can just see her moving dimly.'

After that, Beryl had to have something called Dimly to move.

Dimly does not mind what he is called. He loves the cottage, the garden, the river moving so mysteriously close by and the little noises it makes lapping the banks; he loves the other cats, particularly Elsie. They are the naughty pair. He also likes the foxes.

The cats often commune with the foxes. Bee goes to Berwick Market for rabbit to cook for the cats. What is left over she puts out for the foxes, though young Billy is a great one for seeing the foxes off.

But some nights the cats sit in a circle with the foxes. It is an amazing sight. Beryl watches from the windows of the cottage. Sometimes when the weather is very wintery, her garden becomes a haven in the snow for wild creatures – water-rats, seagulls, voles, mice, the habitual garden birds and the cats – all feeding together, sharing the food she puts out.

Early, very early, one morning, Dimly thought he would help Bee with the shopping. It involved quite a bit of manoeuvring, particularly getting it through the cat flap. Dimly sat under the bureau with his offering, looking sleek and velvety, purring with pride.

Beryl got up to go to the loo in her nightdress. She was confronted by Dimly, guarding an enormous live rabbit under the bureau.

She knew she had to deal with the situation firmly but tactfully. She did not want a slaughtering on her carpet.

'Oh Dimly – what a clever boy; goodness, gracious me, what a lovely rabbit!' she enthused. She hadn't won a Tony Award for nothing.

Dimly did a victory-growl through gritted teeth, his eyes glinting with pleasure. Beryl acted swiftly. She scooped the rabbit up into her arms, turning on her heel. There was no time to stop and dress.

She marched barefoot, nightie floating around her, out into the garden and down the lane, all ten cats following like the Pied Piper; they were wondering where she was taking their breakfast or if this was a new game.

'Oh, what a lovely rabbit! Clever boy, clever Dimly,' she kept saying, but Dimly wasn't fooled.

He ran ahead, miaowing. He loved her, but what was she going to do with his rabbit?

She had to walk quite a long way to find a flat piece of ground with nearby cover. Her feet were wet; her nightie trailed damply, clinging round her ankles. The early morning breeze was cool and she shivered.

'I know it's difficult for you to understand, Dimly,' she said. 'But I can't cook this wild rabbit for you. I'll go tomorrow and buy you a proper rabbit from the market.'

She put down the rabbit, who couldn't believe his luck and shot off into the woods. Then she made a great fuss of Dimly. She did not want him to feel hurt or that his gift had been tossed aside.

Dimly knows Bee will do anything for her cats. He knows about the time Lulu decided to live on the roof and Bee had to climb a ladder several times a day to feed her. Lulu was definitely a little eccentric. When it was snowing, she slept snuggled against the chimney, glad of its warmth.

When Beryl's neighbours had their pine trees chopped down, it became apparent that these trees had been Lulu's access to the roof of the cottage. Lulu promptly disappeared in distress.

This was worrying, so Beryl got a man from the Forestry Commission to cut down a branch of the willow, and they built a little run up onto the roof for Lulu, with slats in the branch for her claws to get a grip on.

But by then Lulu had gone off living on the roof. She had taken up residence elsewhere but couldn't get home because of the stream. So Beryl built a cat-bridge, heaving concrete blocks and wooden planks with her own hands. Now Lulu comes across the Bridge Over the River Kwai for her meals and a talk and a cuddle.

When she is doing this thing called filming, Dimly knows that Bee has to get up very early. The cats don't mind at all. Breakfast at dawn is always acceptable.

But there are so many of them and they all like to eat different foods. Bee usually finds herself tripping over their tails as they mill around the kitchen, desperately trying to remember what each cat is fed on.

'I know you think I'm stupid,' she says to them. 'But I am having to force my brain to work at a very early hour. I suppose Billy and Clive want some red meat. My butcher's making a fortune out of you. It costs more to feed you cats than it does to feed myself.'

They did not like it when she went away filming in America, or doing a play on Broadway. Did she really have to go away to play? There were plenty of bent twigs and little balls of Bacofoil to play with at Honeypot Cottage. She didn't have to get out those dreaded suitcases and pack.

When she went away for a long time to do *The Killing of Sister George*, they showed their displeasure by refusing to come into the cottage when she returned. They sat outside, stiff with disapproval and hurt. It took Bee a long time to win back their trust and love. One by one they gave in to her patient coaxing and returned to the fold.

Dimly often sits on the window seat with Bee when she gets out all her shoes; he loves to play with laces and straps and buckles.

'I have to find the right pair,' she explains to him. 'Before I get into a character, I have to have the right pair of shoes.'

Not being a shoe-wearer, Dimly does not really understand. Bee uses lots of words he does not understand . . . films, plays, theatre, television, parts, scripts, engagements. He just knows she is always busy and always going away. But she has lovely infectious laughter and dimples at the corners of her mouth that go in and out like sunshine.

Dimly is the adventurous one. He obeys the command 'sit and stay'; he will retrieve a Bacofoil ball and bring it back. He caught his leg in a trap and had to have eleven stitches, but he was the perfect invalid and endured the inactivity with dignity.

When he disappeared Beryl became very worried. It was so unlike him; Dimly always came when he was called. He was a lovely cat and they had a special rapport. It made her feel sick to think of something happening to her midnight cat.

She called and called but Dimly did not appear. She searched for three days. She began to feel desperate; she was up at 5 a.m. on the Sunday morning, looking everywhere and calling.

About midday she gave up searching and called a friend in Chatham who is a clairvoyant.

'It's something connected with water,' her friend said after a while. 'He's shut in. Is there a boatyard near you?'

'Nobody's there just now,' said Beryl. 'I don't think he could be shut in there.'

She phoned her friend again on the Monday morning because Dimly had still not returned home, and by now she was distraught. She had hardly slept.

'Get dressed, Beryl, and go round to the boatyard now. I'm quite certain that's where he is.'

Beryl hurried round to the boatyard, followed by Sir Harry and Muriel. She had not wanted them to come because it meant going along a main road. But they insisted. The two cats were miaowing all the time, as if they too were calling for Dimly.

'Oh do be quiet,' she told them eventually. 'Because I won't know if I hear Dimly.'

She searched in all the boats and then looked into a locked shed. There among the shadows was Dimly. He began to cry, a thin pathetic mew as he recognised her voice.

She talked to him all the time as she wondered how she was going to get him out. The door was padlocked; the glass had metal bars and chicken wire behind it. Breaking the glass would not help.

Dimly heard her, so near and yet so far. He could not understand why she was not letting him out. He clawed at the door, his nails rasping.

Beryl was determined. She was going to get her cat out somehow, even if she had to take the shed to pieces. She found an iron bar and with a strength born out of desperation, she levered up the bottom of the door. She is not a big woman and it took every ounce of her strength.

She could feel perspiration breaking out on her face as she strained against the strong door.

Dimly's head appeared through the gap. She gasped with relief, holding the gap open just long enough for a much thinner Dimly to slither out. There was much rejoicing. They all hurried home, Dimly racing ahead; he was starving. But every now and again he stopped to see if Bee was following.

'I'm coming, I'm coming,' she called, getting her breath back, suddenly aware how dry her mouth had been and how her heart had been pumping.

They made a triumphant return to Honeypot Cottage; to its circular rooms and gardens that sweep down to the Thames; to the welcoming committee of cats waiting around for them, tails waving, purring in unison.

At the Lyric Theatre, Shaftesbury Avenue, sat Fleur, a skinny pink-and-brown-patched short-haired cat. She sat at the top of the stairs that lead down to the dressing rooms, ignored and unloved. No one ever took any notice of her. There was a streak of Abyssinian in the bony head and pointed ears; her eyes were wary as if she had once been booted down the stairs or out into the streets.

Fleur did not know that a star was coming into her life who would change it. A woman who would bring her cooked food fresh from home; who would send out for turkey sandwiches, break them up and feed them to her from an ashtray; who would let her sleep safely on the divan in her dressing room.

Dimly could have told the thin theatre cat that all this would happen when *Gigi* opened in London, and she would soon become one of those fortunate creatures – a member of Bee's family of cats.

Cloud Eight

It was a forbidden place. A cold white box with the faint hum of machinery. But it held a fascination for Victcha. She often sat outside its door, waiting patiently, knowing it housed all sorts of delicacies – chicken, liver, milk, cream, cheese, trifle, butter . . . Victcha almost drooled in anticipation. Even her favourite Whiskas used to live in there if she happened to leave any – which was not often.

Victcha was not sure of the sequence of events that gave her access to this holy of holies, but perhaps someone left the door open or the catch slipped. It was about five feet high, free standing; it was easy to miss a small black and white shape crouched on a back shelf hopefully impersonating a carton of juice. Then someone shut the door without seeing the cat.

It was very dark inside and the hum was louder now. Victcha explored the shelf. It seemed to be almost empty. Only some bottles and boxes. Where had all the lovely food gone? She sniffed expectantly. But everything was covered up.

It was also cold inside, a fact which did not bother Victcha at first. Her coat kept her warm. She huddled, flipping her tail over her nose. The tips of her ears were paper thin and beginning to feel cold. It was a sensation she did not like.

She curled herself into a smaller ball, wishing the cold would go away. It was not such a nice place after all. She grew restless and scratched at the door, miaowing. No one heard.

Sleep was coming over her in waves. Instinctively she fought off the sleepiness, knowing that this was not a normal sleep.

'Victcha . . . Victcha . . .'

She heard her name, very faint and far away.

She was trembling now, an ague over which she had no control. It was becoming difficult to breathe as the cold began to paralyse her muscles. She could not fight the overwhelming sleepiness.

She was floating. It was a strange weightlessness, as if she was made of air. She did not question her new state because it was not frightening and she felt very un-curious.

There were dreams in her mind. It was like spinning back to when she was a kitten and the world was very new. Images floated in and out of her consciousness, vague but recognisable, comforting and not in any way a threat.

The cold was something she had never endured before, but it no longer mattered. She had gone beyond the point of feeling the cold; she was frozen; but the pain had gone.

The mist was a strange colour now; lavender, rose and blue, very blue . . . it was the sky, a vast endless sky, above, below and all around her.

'Her heart has stopped beating,' said the vet, Dennis Archer. 'It's not surprising. How long was she trapped in the fridge?'

'We're not sure. But she was missing for up to twenty-four hours.'

'There's not much hope, then.'

'Can't you try? Please try. There could be a chance,'

urged Dorothy Wozniak. Her little black and white cat was the joy of her life. 'Please do something.'

Mr Archer tried to find the heart-beat eight times, but eventually gave up. Victcha remained icy cold. There was an odd gasp from the still form.

'I'm sorry, but she's technically dead of hypothermia.'

Dorothy was heart-broken. Her lovely little cat. They left Victcha lying on the vet's table, thinking they would never see her again.

'Look,' said Mr Archer. 'Her temperature is too low to record. But I will give her an anti-shock injection, and put her in a kennel with warm blankets and an infra-red light. If there's no change in the morning, then I'll make all the arrangements to dispose of the body.'

He always hated this part but someone had to be practical. Sometimes a grieving owner preferred to take their pet back to a familiar garden; others did not want a painful reminder.

The young art student went home with her family. They would never know how Victcha had got shut in the fridge. They could not forgive themselves for allowing it to happen. But the refrigerator was the last place they had thought of looking for Victcha when she went missing.

What a pity, thought Mr Archer, preparing the injection. It was a nicely marked cat with a sweet white face and big patches of black above the eyes and under the jaw. The cat would not have known much about it, or suffered. It would have got progressively colder, then simply gone to sleep. But he did as he had promised and left the cat under an infra-red lamp.

It was another busy day at the surgery; cats and dogs of all shapes and sizes came and went. Mr Archer was called out several times.

It was seven hours after Victcha had been brought into the surgery when a veterinary assistant, working late, heard a funny noise. The black and white cat had thrown off the blanket and was getting unsteadily to her feet, looking around in a dazed manner. Victcha shook her head, wondering where she was. She stretched her stiff limbs and began to stagger to the edge of the kennel.

'Good heavens,' exclaimed the assistant. 'She's alive! It's a miracle.'

Victcha began to miaow feebly. She was feeling hollow and hungry and still cold. The tips of her ears were tingling like ice.

The assistant heated some milk and Victcha lapped the warm drink gratefully. She was emerging from the strangest dreams. She could not make out what was real. They were fading now as the world became a familiar place again. The assistant wrapped her in a blanket and stroked her.

'There, pussy. You have had a strange adventure.'

'I can't believe it,' said Mr Archer, examining the cat thoroughly in the morning. 'That cat was technically dead. No heart-beat. Temperature too low to record. The odd gasp. Nothing. Somehow she's come back to life. As you say, it's a miracle.'

The Wozniak household was wrapped in gloom. They were all upset about the fate of their little cat. Victcha had meant a lot to them.

'I think I'll just ring the vet's, once more,' said Dorothy.

She listened in amazement, hardly able to believe her ears, trying to take in what the receptionist was telling her.

'It's Victcha! She's alive after all. She suddenly came back to life and started staggering around. She's all right now and we can go round and collect her any time.'

Dorothy's eyes filled with tears of joy. Her prayers to St Francis of Assisi had been answered.

Victcha came home to much rejoicing, though she did not understand what had happened. She had gone to sleep in one place and somehow woken up in another. It was all very peculiar.

She has fully recovered but is a little wary of the refrigerator now. Despite the memories of lovely food inside it, she knows it holds the cold hand of death.

Ad Infinitum

The two new kittens, Clover and Rufus, did not get into a story, despite persistent cajoling. They were among the dozens of cats that did not quite make a story of their own. Big, small, funny, brave, strange, sad . . . each cat an individual character and special to its owner.

'Please do something,' the provider urged. 'Anything so I can use you. After all, I do know all about you. I ought to be able to write a good story about you two.'

'We're trying, we're trying,' they chorused.

'I did get stuck up a tree,' said Clover, the tortoiseshell kitten with a mascara-smudged face and two clown's teardrops under her big dark eyes. 'I was terribly frightened.'

'It was a very small tree and you were only stuck up it for about five minutes. I'd hardly call that a world-shattering event.'

'But my mistress also got stuck up the tree trying to get me down,' Clover went on. 'Surely that's worth a line?'

'Okay, a line. A line. But that's all you're getting.'

A brown black and white tabby called Corgi from Horley was rescued from a fire in a burning flat in Fulham. Somehow his half-burnt vaccination book survived the fire too. Corgi is now a massive twenty-pound twelve-year-old with a penchant for playing badminton and climbing into upstairs bedrooms via a handy fir tree.

Since 1981 Corgi has had diabetes and endures regular insulin injections. He is quite used to the routine and at the same time each evening sits on a dining-room chair waiting for his injection.

And the rescue from the fire? Only Corgi knows the details of that terrifying experience.

A brave cat called Smokey killed a snake in New Guinea, while Pepsi survived fifteen minutes in a washing machine and lived to produce her own kitten later.

From long ago comes the story of Pongo, the sea captain's cat who shared his master's cabin. In Alexandria Pongo took extended shore leave and the ship had to sail without him. A year later, in Cardiff, the captain was walking along the docks when a cargo vessel berthed. On board he saw his cat, Pongo. The mutual delight of their reunion can be imagined. Had the cat been searching for him, in the only way he knew?

Do cats cry? It seems that some do. A cat sat by the grave of a kitten crying for five minutes.

A cat called Sooty had to have a passport, pawprints and full description, before flying out of Aden. Another cat, Ponsonby, knew to the day when its owner was returning from a month in Japan.

Percy is a ginger cat who was brought up with a cat flap, but when the family moved, there was only a door with a letter box. Percy soon learned to use the knocker on the letter-box to ask to be let in. It became a family joke to send visitors to answer any knock at the door.

'They're lovely stories,' said Clover. 'Look, we're both sitting in your shopping basket, impersonating the cover on a calendar. Don't we look cute? Does that make a story?'

'No, sorry. Get out.'

There's an eccentric cat called Twit who once went swimming in engine oil and had to be bathed in the sink to get it off; he also sits under the village bus until rescued and swims in the bath.

Victoria is a cat who likes Ovaltine and whisky. She walked into the house and stayed eighteen years, a black and white Persian who can definitely play the piano.

A little tortoiseshell called Streaky was accidentally locked in a TV delivery van and driven away, but somehow travelled back the six miles to her home on her own over totally unknown main roads.

Billy, an active twelve-year-old living in Chesterfield, disappeared unaccountably one evening. Eight weeks later the mother and son in the family separately heard his special mew, asking to be let in. Though they searched the yard and the garden, Billy was nowhere to be found. They did not say anything to each other, hiding their disappointment. But years later, talking about Billy, they both mentioned the mewing they had heard that evening.

It made them wonder if Billy was trapped by cat thieves and the calls they heard so clearly were when their cat died.

There's a happier ending to the story of Basil, who swallowed a diamond engagement ring and had to have a £95 operation to remove it.

'I didn't mind about the loss of the ring. It was Basil I was worried about,' said his owner.

At this point, the kitten Clover curled herself round the provider's ankles. 'We eat all sorts of strange things,' she purred hopefully. 'Raw cake mixture, chocolate, sultanas, Christmas pudding.'

'We must be the only spinach-eating cats in Great Britain,' said the solemn kitten Rufus, speaking for the first time. He's a wise cat, this tawny fluffy lion with sleepy yellow eyes. He seldom wastes time on talking, except when climbing up the provider's leg to see what she is chopping for their supper.

'That's it. That's definitely worth a story,' said Clover, dancing away to chase a bumble-bee over the rockery, her thistledown mind already on something else. 'Spinach and liver. I love spinach and liver . . .'

There are countless tales of cats returning to their old homes when the family has moved to a new house. Tabs, a Portsmouth pussy, made such dreadful wailing noises night and day outside her old home that the neighbours had to call in the RSPCA to catch the homesick cat and return her to her owners. She was so cold and hungry that she decided to make the best of the move and rarely ventured out again.

Many owners believe that their cats speak to them. Fluffy, of Aristotle Road, London, seemed to speak quite clearly. He was a long-haired stray with the exotic make-up of a ballet dancer, whose gaze showed compassion, humour and an analytical approach to everything that went on around him. His owner is sure that there was some mental telepathy between them.

The cashier cat lives on a farm in north-west Yorkshire. The farm sells free-range eggs to passing motorists. On one occasion, as a customer held out a pound note to pay for eggs, the big ginger cat reached out from a bench, got hold of the note in its mouth and ran inside the farmhouse with it. The cat gave its trophy to the farmer's wife and went back to its seat in the porch.

Nor was it the first time. Some weeks previously Ginger had fished a £5 note out of the handbag of a customer who was trying to find some change.

A tiger tabby called Sir Henry fairly froze with astonishment when he saw a near life-size coloured painting of his owners newly hung on a wall. He looked in amazement from the painting to his owners and back again, investigated the frame, in and around it thoroughly. Reassured that they were not really hanging on the wall, he has totally ignored the picture ever since.

Sir Henry wheedled his way into the life and home of a pilot who was in Bomber Command in World War II, despite the fact that they were not a cat family and had never had a cat before. Sir Henry decided he was going to stay at April Cottage and proceeded to clear the area of all other strays.

He was knighted with a breadknife for his work among the mice. The local vet said he was pleased to have so distinguished a cat as a client.

A Swindon family had three highly intelligent cats, Albertine, Moppet and Flopsy. Albertine had hidden a damaged kitten and would not let anyone know where it was.

Her owner said: 'Oh Albertine, why don't you bring your kitten down? It's so cold up there for a baby.'

Albertine looked earnestly into her face, then ran upstairs, returned with the kitten in her mouth and dumped it onto her owner's lap, as if to say: 'Okay, she's all yours.'

Moppet could not stand her owner singing, particularly high notes and 'Silent Night'. This carol made her react quite fiercely. One night Moppet died and the next morning at school the music teacher chose for assembly . . . 'Silent Night'.

Flopsy had impeccable manners but once attacked the radio when a previously undiscovered musical instrument was demonstrated on Radio 3. The cat went wild. It was an April Fool's Day joke on listeners, but Flopsy had not been fooled.

A true music lover is the phantom cat of the Ohio Theatre, Columbus. This sleek black cat insists on joining in with the Columbus Symphony Orchestra, miaowing in time in an eerie soprano.

So often cats seems to be sent by some divine purpose to help in a situation. This is a beautiful story, almost spine-tingling. A strange tortoiseshell and white cat jumped in a window on a Saturday and made itself quite at home. The two sisters were surprised but pleased to see the cat for its presence comforted them. Their mother was terminally ill and she died the very next day.

The cat stayed with them night and day. When they

returned home from the funeral, the cat had gone, never to return.

The sisters hunted for the cat but without success. Two months later they saw an advertisement about a tortoiseshell cat that had been found. They hurried to see the cat, hoping that it would be the one that had visited them in their time of need, but it was not. However, she was a beautiful lost creature and they took her home. Taff gave them fourteen years of pleasure and they still have Nob, one of her kittens.

One morning Mrs Poole was washing dishes, looking out of the window at the peaceful Wimbleball Reservoir in Somerset, when she saw what looked like a can of baked beans on legs. Four legs. The can was progressing unsteadily across the garden. It was their cat, Tiger, a magnificent tabby, with his head stuck in a tin.

She tried to remove the tin but Tiger had his head hopelessly wedged. She rushed the cat and tin in the car to find the senior warden and another warden. With great care the two men were able to remove the can with a pair of snips.

Tiger made the national newspapers and became a local celebrity.

Tubby is an acrobatic cat who likes nothing better than to be wheelbarrowed round the room on his front legs; he also likes tea, Ovaltine and a tiny drop of Cherry Brandy. He turns his nose up at coffee.

Blackie, the family's other cat, enjoys the daily ritual of sitting in the front passenger seat of the car and being driven into the garage. He likes to eat fruit cake, salty biscuits, dry cornflakes and health-food fruit bars.

A colony of feral cats were inherited by new residents in Via Aschenez in Reggio di Calabria in Italy. On their first morning in the flat, the husband and wife found the ferals sitting outside, expectantly waiting in a semi-circle.

It was a problem – how to feed what amountd to a private zoo. They grew fond of the ferals, but the cats often disappeared or became ill. A female feral brought them her kittens for inspection then took them away. One they called Nelson, a fierce one-eyed creature, was untouchable. But years later, on the day that he died, he lay on top of their wall and allowed them a single stroke. It was probably the only time he had been touched by a human in his long, embattled life.

Lilian, actually a male black cat, lived in the home of the Senior Commissioner of the Gambian Protectorate in Bathurst. This cat's party piece was to be found sitting on the Governor's chair at the head of the table each time there was a formal dinner party. He liked to stroll over the dining table and drink the water from the flower bowls of bougainvillaea and zinnias.

He also loved to chase the house bats that flew down from the roof of their house-on-stilts. Lilian could leap as high as a standard lamp.

He went on safari with the Commissioner and his wife up the Gambia river, and was fast asleep in a thatched wooden guest house when a hoard of warrior ants came out of the jungle. These fierce creatures tunnel their way through everything, attacking and eating all in their path.

Lilian was saved by a boy watchman who lit fires to stop the invading ants and diverted their onslaught. They would have eaten the sleeping cat if they had not been stopped.

'Absolutely fascinating,' said Clover, walking over the provider's typewriter with little dancing steps. 'But you haven't put us in a story yet. Aren't we sweet and funny and amazing? And we eat beetroot, tomatoes, chocolate cake and raisins. We're nearly vegetarians.'

Rufus blinks his amber eyes wisely like an owl. 'Remember how we form a queue for supper? That's well-trained, isn't it?'

'What about when we first arrived and Cindy, our Colourpoint Grandmother, was jealous and ran away?' Clover said, prancing around on top of valuable papers.

'She only ran away as far as next door. We could see

173

her sitting there all day with her back to us,' said the provider, removing the now reconciled fluffy cushion on legs from a pile of typing paper.

'And she went on hunger strike for four days,' Clover reminded her. 'Who went crawling around under furniture with saucers of milk to tempt her?'

'Er . . . yes, well, we won't go into that,' said the provider.

'What about when I fell in the bath?'

'I fell in the frog pond,' Rufus yawned pinkly.

'You certainly did! I didn't expect to have to give you a bath at 1 a.m. in the morning. Green slime everywhere. Urgh.'

The kittens began washing each other's faces. A lick here, a lick there, totally innocent, intent on cleaning up.

'We help you tidy up, don't we?' said Clover, not giving up easily. 'Put things away.'

'You mean hide anything that takes your fancy, like ball-point pens and emery boards. I suppose it could be called tidying up. By the way, where's the top of my new pen?'

'And I'm helping in the garden,' Clover went on. 'I'm bringing in all the rhododendron leaves and taking them upstairs.'

'Thanks a bundle. We don't want the entire garden indoors. Why not try taking them down to the compost heap?'

The kittens ignored the suggestion; that would turn play into work, the last thing they were interested in.

'How about the sweet way I pat your face when you blow on my paws,' says Clover brightly, her little smudged face alight with love.

'Dear baby, that doesn't make a story . . . but thank you for trying. The moment I finish this book, you'll both do something amazing,' said the provider, scooping them into her arms, a gloriously soft mixture of black tortoiseshell and tawny marmalade fur, eight paws waving in the air, two pink noses burrowing into her neck.

'At least I can have the last word,' Clover purred.

'Definitely almost the last word,' agreed Rufus, drawing his huge foxy tail carefully over his eyes and drifting into sleep.